Chasing Blood Money

The Anatomy of Gun Control in America

By

David L. Nelson

Chasing Blood Money, Published November, 2020

Editorial and proofreading services: Kathleen A. Tracy
Interior layout and cover design: Howard Johnson
Photo Credits: Author's photograph supplied by his law firm, Sommers
Schwartz of Southfield, Michigan.
Cover photo: *March for our Lives,* courtesy Tim Brown.

SDP Publishing

Published by SDP Publishing, an imprint of SDP Publishing Solutions, LLC.

To obtain permission(s) to use material from this work, please submit a
written request to:

SDP Publishing
Permissions Department
PO Box 26, East Bridgewater, MA 02333
or email your request to info@SDPPublishing.com.

ISBN-13 (print): 978-1-7343317-5-2
ISBN-13 (ebook): 978-1-7343317-6-9

Library of Congress Control Number: 2020916700

Printed in the United States of America

This book is dedicated to the victims of gun violence at Columbine, Sandy Hook, and Stoneman Douglas, and to victims of mass shootings across the nation and to their families and loved ones.

ACKNOWLEDGMENTS

The librarian at the author's law firm, Mary Margaret Serpento, contributed a great deal of her time, editing, and research skills as well as her suggestions and advice to the completion of this manuscript. My legal assistant, Kimberly Kortes, devoted her superb computer skills to organizing, formatting and reformatting the manuscript. Mr. Adam Winn, as a senior law student at the Wayne State University Law School, and senior articles editor of the *Wayne Law Review*, researched the legal authorities and cite-checked them. Dr. Rebecca Nelson, a grammarian now teaching at the University of Nebraska at Kearney who has studied and teaches dialects, discourse, and sociolinguistics, assisted me in understanding the grammatical structure of the Second Amendment. My brother, Frederick J. Nelson, who taught engineering technology at the University of Toledo, read the manuscript while it was being prepared for publication and made suggestions that substantially improved it. Lisa Akoury Ross of SDP Publishing Solutions molded the manuscript into book form. Kathleen A. Tracy edited the manuscript and greatly improved it. I would also like to acknowledge and thank the many newspaper writers, editors, and photographers whose articles, editorials, and photography provided a continuous stream of background data.

Finally, I thank my wife, Judith Nelson, for her patience, advice, and assistance throughout the process of completing the manuscript; my daughter Julie, who has a master's degree in fine arts from Goddard College in Vermont, for inspiring me to write this book and advising me on matters of style and grammar; and my sons David and Daniel for setting up my home computer and creating computer files to contain the manuscript as it was assembled.

TABLE OF CONTENTS

A well-regulated militia, being necessary to the security of a free State, the right of the people to keep and bear Arms, shall not be infringed.

—*Second Amendment to the Constitution of the United States*

We live in a world of nuclear giants and ethical infants, in a world that has achieved brilliance without wisdom, power without conscience. We have solved the mystery of the atom and forgotten the Sermon on the Mount. We know more about war than we know about peace, more about dying than we know about living.

—*Gen. Omar N. Bradley*

I will give up my gun when they peel my cold dead fingers from around it.

—*Citizens Committee for the Right to Keep and Bear Arms bumper sticker*

In the absence of a Congress ready to act to reduce gun violence, we will keep working to create a different Congress.

—*Gabrielle Giffords*

INTRODUCTION

A dramatic upheaval of the law.
— *Justice John Paul Stevens*

The militias that safeguarded colonial America and created our nation, followed by our long history with private gun ownership for hunting, recreation, and self-defense, have nurtured a belief among many Americans that the private ownership and carriage of firearms is a natural right that no government can take away. This belief was reinforced over time by war, federal and state legislative inertia, a burgeoning trade in weapons with escalating firepower, paid lobbyists, and by decisions emanating from our highest court. Bottom line: Guns are imbedded in our culture.

This culture encourages the private carriage of firearms, believes that the answer to gun violence is a good guy with a gun, and abhors even the most innocuous regulation. Grounded in the right of self-defense savage gun violence manifests itself as suicide, domestic violence, mass murder, school shootings, disabling injury, billions of dollars wasted, and families torn apart. Cemented into constitutional law, its reality confronts any who seek balanced, common sense gun regulation. Left unanswered is whether the private right to bear arms that our Supreme Court drew from the Second Amendment threatens the rule of law and the continued existence of our republic. Other constitutional issues divide our electorate but none more fundamental or deep-rooted than the right to bear arms.

My research for this book became a quest to understand the forces that drive the gun debate. What do those who promote a right to bear arms seek? What do they fear? What are the limits of the right? Is common sense regulation even possible? Clippings were cut and stored in boxes, and text written and revised, but it languished in Word—the musings of a retired lawyer. Congressional debate had stalled. Viewpoints all over the political spectrum flooded the news media with statistics, horrific video footage, and angry editorials on a daily basis. What more could be said? No matter what, nothing was going to happen. Why bother to write and publish another book about any of that?

Then the tectonic plates supporting the gun control debate shifted. From the epicenter at Marjory Stoneman Douglas High School in Parkland, Florida, shockwaves rippled through Washington, D.C. and across the nation. They roared across the pages of this manuscript. Thousands of energized school students were marching for gun control. Would that make a difference? Would Congress or our states finally enact common sense gun laws? What would they look like? While this manuscript was being rewritten, critiqued, and updated, gun violence statistics continued to pour out of the media. Still, the nation did little more than watch and listen. Our law-givers kept their collective heads in the sand. Even legislation to expand Brady background checks remained tabled.

But the forces driving the gun debate did not take a holiday. On Monday, August 5, 2019, headlines blared out:

ONE SHOOTING MASSACRE FOLLOWS ANOTHER SHAKING A BEWILDERED NATION TO ITS ROOTS.

A gunman, alleged to be the author of a manifesto protesting illegal immigration, had opened fire at a Walmart supermarket in El Paso Texas, killing 22 people and wounding dozens more.[1] Thirteen hours later another gunman armed with a semiautomatic killed 9 persons and wounded over 20 others outside a bar in Dayton, Ohio.[2]

America has failed to establish common sense gun control even though it endures gun violence at a level far beyond that in the rest of the civilized world. Many of our citizens revere private gun ownership and refuse to be regulated. Manufacturers and dealers enjoy lucrative gun sales profits generated from that reverence. Political leaders supported by lobbyists and campaign contributions build careers promoting the rights of gun owners. When asked, the Supreme Court found a right to bear arms in the Second Amendment but failed to define its limits. As a consequence, criminals, terrorists, and those unfit to have them can acquire, carry, and use firearms.

When Supreme Court Justice Antonin Scalia wrote the majority opinion in *District of Columbia v. Heller*[3] holding that the Second Amendment set forth a private right to bear arms, he exposed a seismic fault line in government "of the people, by the people, and for the people." That fault line, running through other issues confronting the nation, has become a disturbing echo of the events leading to the American Civil War. The gulf between those who champion a right to bear arms and those who seek gun control grows ever wider. While powerful interests shunt aside legislated solutions, the number and power of firearms keeps growing, and the dead keep piling up. As of 2017 there were over 357 million firearms in the United States—about 1.13 guns for each person—many of them semiautomatic rifles and handguns in the possession of the emotionally or mentally unstable, or criminally minded.[4]

Justice Scalia wrote in *Heller*, "It is not the role of this Court to pronounce the Second Amendment extinct."[5] However, as we shall see, the fault line through the national debate on gun control runs right through the Second Amendment itself. Historically, the Court never claimed a power to strike the words *well-regulated militia* from the Second Amendment, nor did it claim it had power to deprive Congress or state legislatures of their power to regulate guns. Intended or not, *Heller* separated firearms into two categories. One consists of weapons suitable for military use, and the other firearms suitable for private civilian use. Because of the highly destructive power of modern military weapons, there is no serious opposition to regulating the military's use of explosive devices and firearms. Express provisions of the Constitution and the military command structure provide for that. But after *Heller* where does the line between military weapons and civilian firearms fall? *Heller* did not tell us.

To find a civilian right to own and carry firearms in the Constitution, *Heller* laid aside the well-regulated militia language contained in the Second Amendment. In its place the Court announced the right to be a *not unlimited*[6] right belonging only to *law-abiding, responsible citizens*.[7] Each of these concepts is difficult to grasp let alone enforce and particularly so when the restraining words *well-regulated* are taken away. Other constitutional rights such as freedom of speech, freedom of religion, and the right to not incriminate oneself don't have a law-abiding citizen qualifier. Those rights belong to all citizens good and bad. Placing a private right to bear arms alongside those rights reveals it does not belong there. It's different because firearms and explosive devices deliver mass murder, devastation, and grave injury in seconds. Perpetrators can't walk back cold-blooded murder, suicide, or disabling injury like they can speech. Common sense dictates that any right to bear arms, military or civilian, calls out for responsible regulation. That said, *Heller* is now the law of the land. Its holding and its limitations must be dealt with.

For the first 220 years of our nation's history it was believed, though strongly opposed, that the right to bear arms described in the Second Amendment did not create a private constitutional right to bear arms. Until 2008 the amendment was seen as providing only a right to bear arms for military uses that would be well-regulated. Overturning and explaining away prior decisions of the Court that read the amendment that way, Justice Scalia's majority opinion in *Heller* announced that the first phrase of the Second Amendment did *not* restrict the second clause, and that the Second Amendment did, indeed, provide a private right to bear arms for nonmilitary uses that belongs to law-abiding, responsible citizens, *stare decisis*[*] be damned and no matter what prior Court opinions may have held.

The original intent of the Founding Fathers as read from the text of the Constitution itself, he wrote, compelled that result.[8] Even though Justice Scalia modified the private right to bear arms as being not unlimited,[9] his opinion shifted the tectonic plates. Some gun rights advocates didn't see their new right as limited and vociferously pressed for the right to carry semiautomatic firearms with high capacity magazines and bump stocks and to open carry in public places like schools and churches. *Heller* handed them a powerful argument. Four Justices dissented. One of them, the late Justice John Paul Stevens, described Justice Scalia's opinion as a "dramatic upheaval of the law."[10] Subsequent events confirm Stevens's view.

The nation is now struggling to define the private right to bear arms that Justice Scalia drew from the Second Amendment. How does the nation segregate law-abiding, responsible citizens from those unfit and from terrorists? How do we separate military firearms and explosives not encompassed within the private right

---

[*]A Latin phrase that means *to stand by that which is decided*. When a court makes a decision, it establishes a legal precedent that is used by subsequent courts in their deliberations. In so doing, they are applying the legal doctrine of *stare decisis*, considered one of the most important doctrines in Western law.

to bear arms from civilian firearms that are? How do we identify and protect the places where the right may not be exercised? How do we accomplish any of that while immersed in a fierce fight funded by deep pockets and raging within the electorate?

The issues are hardly academic. Bloody, agonizing tragedies arising from gun violence confront our nation daily. The FBI's annual *Crime in the United States* for 2016 reported that 1,248,185 violent crimes were committed within the United States that year,[11] 17,250 of them murders, with firearms accounting for 73 percent of the homicides. Gunshot victims and grief-stricken survivors are more than statistics; they are the gruesome aftermath when firearms deprive real people of life, liberty, and the pursuit of happiness.

The debate should not be about parsing words or clauses found in the Second Amendment. It should be about people and the quality of life in America. Following the brutal killing of 17 people and the wounding of 15 others at Marjory Stoneman Douglas High School in Parkland, Florida, on Valentine's Day 2018 by a disturbed shooter armed with an AR-15 semiautomatic rifle, *The New York Times* printed comments from Stoneman Douglas students. The quarterback on the football team, who had escaped, spoke of assistant football coach Aaron Feis, who also served as the school security guard and sat at the school gate each morning in a golf cart, giving arriving kids thumbs up. Feis had been shot and killed.

"He cared about us as people, not just as football players."

I love you, Coach, the quarterback recalled saying to Feis that Valentine's Day morning.

"I love you, too, bub," Feis replied. "I'll see you at 2:30."[12]

These are the simple, commonplace words people who like and respect each other use every day in America, but you know from reading them that Coach Feis had been a beloved man. Coach Feis is but one of thousands of beautiful lives taken from us by senseless gun violence.

If the *Heller* opinion was intended to solve our gun problem by promoting a theory that an armed citizenry asserting their right to self-defense would deter gun violence, it has failed. Congress did nothing, not even after Stoneman Douglas, and the pace of school shootings quickened. Another school shooting occurred at a high school in Santa Fe, Texas, on May 18, 2018. Reports said ten were killed and ten wounded.[13] School shootings had become commonplace and school children were being taught survival techniques. The issue is not whether *Heller* increased the level of gun violence as some may ask. No detailed studies have been located to tell us definitely whether *Heller* increased or decreased gun violence. The studies we do have (see discussion in Chapter 1) tell us that gun violence existed at unacceptable levels prior to and after *Heller.* Our nation is an outlier on gun control, enabling firearm savagery that makes the gunplay of the Mafia's heyday look almost quaint. The issue after *Heller* (and later *McDonald*) is whether those opinions and political realities have unduly restricted the power of Congress and state legislatures to enact effective gun control when it is clear rational control is needed.

This book describes the historical and political antecedents of our gun culture, explores early Supreme Court decisions interpreting the Second Amendment, and analyzes recent Supreme Court decisions that dramatically changed Second Amendment law to permit the private ownership and carriage of firearms. Existing federal and state statutes and past legislative efforts to achieve gun control are presented to demonstrate they fail to provide an adequate legal structure for dealing with gun violence in our nation. Homicide, suicide, domestic violence in the home, mass shootings, school shootings, and terrorism are chronicled here to clarify the issues new legislation must address. This book also examines political realities and the corrosive impact that another Supreme Court decision, *Citizens United v. Federal Election Commission,* has had on the politics of gun control. It describes Constitutional provisions that provide Congress and our states with power to bring gun violence under control and suggests specific new gun control laws. Many books, articles and op-ed pieces describe in much greater detail than attempted here the history of the right to bear arms in England and the colonies, the antecedents of colonial militias, the writings of the colonists who drafted the Second Amendment, court decisions prior to 2008, the *Heller* and *McDonald* decisions, gun violence statistics, the political aspects of gun rights and gun control, and the activities of gun rights lobbyists. *The Second Amendment: A Biography,* by Michael Waldman (2014) is an excellent example. The Further Reading section lists other titles below—some criticize the right to bear arms and others explain and justify the need for such a right.

Several types of firearms are referred to in this book. The following brief description, though rendered in layman's terms and far from complete, provides a bird's eye view of the evolving types of firearms manufactured, owned, and borne in America.

- In colonial times colonists used muzzle loaded guns that were slow to load manually, single shot, and had poor accuracy.

- Powder and ball guns were later replaced by guns firing single "cartridges," which contained both the bullet and powder in one device. Barrel rifling was introduced to improve accuracy.

- Simple single shot cartridge guns were later replaced by "repeating" guns into which multiple cartridges could be loaded at one time. After firing one bullet, a mechanical device such as a lever or pump action slide was used to eject the spent cartridge and introduce a fresh one into the firing chamber. Multiple bullets could be rapidly fired until the supply in the gun was used up, at which time the gun was manually reloaded.

- Later, clips were invented to eliminate the problem of loading one cartridge at a time. A clip could be preloaded with cartridges and the entire clip could be inserted into the gun. When spent, the clip could be replaced with a new clip in seconds. Originally, clips contained less than ten rounds. They now contain many more.

- Then, instead of ejecting spent cartridges mechanically, guns were modified such that hot gases in the firing chamber would eject a spent cartridge and a spring mechanism would load a new cartridge into the firing chamber. A pistol, shotgun, or rifle so equipped could be fired as rapidly as the shooter could pull the trigger, one bullet at a time, until all of the cartridges loaded into the gun were fired. The gun still had to be reloaded either manually or with a fresh clip and was thought of as being "semiautomatic," but it required separate trigger pulls to discharge each cartridge.

- Along the way, fully automatic hand-held weapons were introduced, known as machine guns, which allowed the weapon to keep firing with a single pull of the trigger until all available cartridges loaded into the magazine of the weapon were fired. In 1934 Congress taxed the sale of machine guns and in 1965 it enacted laws that made the manufacture and sale of machine guns unlawful. These laws did not outlaw machine guns already owned on the date of enactment.

- To avoid legislated restrictions on machine guns, devices such as expanded magazines, trigger activators and bump stocks were invented to increase the firing rate of semi-automatic weapons to emulate that of a machine gun.

While this book probes into some of that history and background and provides the author's own critique of laws and opinions supporting the right to bear arms, the purpose here is not to restate history. Rather, this book leaves the mind-bending historical and grammatical justification for the Court's decision in *Heller* and its ultimate fate to others. What it seeks to address are the bloody consequences that came after *Heller* and what those of us who live in the here and now can do to alleviate them. It aims to demonstrate that existing constitutional, statutory, and court-made law are incapable of controlling the carnage currently being inflicted upon innocent civilians from highly dangerous firearms in the hands of those unfit to have them, and that it is time to move on.

The goal of this book is to aid those who seek laws to rein in the avalanche of firearms burying our nation. It is not intended to be a legal or scholarly treatise, although the legal issues are there and need to be discussed. It asks gun rights advocates to look at the laws we have and don't have and to come to the table. Although a uniform, national gun control law will meet fierce resistance, all of us need to take a hard look at our history with guns and face the nightmarish power of modern firearms. It's time we study gun control laws in other nations. It's time we adopt principled, rational firearms and explosives control laws within the parameters of the United States Constitution. It's time to rein in the violence, death, and destruction guns produce.

It is most assuredly way past time for that.

CHAPTER 1

A Uniquely American Gun Culture

All you need for happiness is a good gun, a good horse, and a good wife.
— *Daniel Boone*

Our history with guns is very different from that of other civilized nations. The 2011 *Small Arms Survey*, an annual review of global small arms issues, featured a chart estimating the top ten countries for civilian firearms.[1] The report based the estimate on known registrations, household surveys, expert estimates, and other sources. The survey estimated that of the 875 million firearms then in existence, civilian firearm ownership world-wide was approximately 650 million. Even with the qualifier that exact numbers were unavailable, the numbers are shocking:

United States	270 million
India	46 million
China	40 million
Germany	25 million
Pakistan	18 million
Mexico	15.5 million
Brazil	14.8 million
Russia	12.75 million
Yemen	11.5 million
Thailand	10 million
Others	186 million

Based on these estimates, over 40 percent of all firearms in civilian hands worldwide are located in the United States, even though as of 2016 only about 4 percent of the world's population lived in the United States.[2] On a per capita basis, the private ownership of firearms in the United States exceeds the worldwide average by a factor of ten. That number directly correlates to data from the Gun Violence Archive on reported incidents of gun violence in the United States for 2017[3] —on average 38 people died and another 81 were wounded *daily*. Gun violence data for 2017 and 2018 compiled by the Gun Violence Archive, not including suicide, is as follows:

	2017	2018
Total number of incidents:	61,590	57,391
Number of deaths:	15,612	14,773
Number of injuries:	31,263	28,237
Mass shootings:	346	340
Children killed or injured:	733	669
Teens killed or injured:	3,256	2850
Officers shot or killed:	311	283
Suspects shot or killed by police:	2,081	2,137

When all deaths during 2017 also include suicides, the number of deaths totals 39,773. An estimated total of 1.625 million civilians have died from gunfire in America since 1968. American deaths from firearms for 1994 totaled approximately 37,500—the year the federal statute that banned semiautomatics and extended loading devices took effect. By 2004 American deaths from firearms fell to approximately 31,000—the year that the semiautomatic and extended loading device ban expired. The year the *Heller* case was decided, 2008, American deaths from firearms totaled approximately 32, 000. After the 2008 Heller decision the total deaths of Americans by firearms increased annually for the next nine years. By 2017 the total American deaths from firearms had climbed to 39,773 as shown above. No direct evidence proves that the expiration of the semiautomatic and extended loading device ban or that the *Heller* or *Macdonald* decisions created this increase, but the increase is there, and those events certainly did not prevent it.[4]

John Donohue, a law professor at Stanford Law School, assisted by a Stanford law student, studied mortality rates produced by assault weapons in mass murders. He concluded that the 1994 assault weapons ban worked. He found that mass shootings dropped during the assault weapons ban and that a 347 percent increase in fatalities in gun massacres occurred after the ban expired, even as the overall violent crime rate went down. He stated as follows in a *New York Times* op ed: "Indeed, if we continue at the post-2014 pace, by 2024 we will have had more than 10 times as many gun massacre deaths in that 10 year period as we had during the decade of the federal assault weapons ban."[5]

These are not idle statistics we can shove into a file. As a result of our history with private gun ownership, semiautomatics, extended loading devices, and weak gun laws, Americans live in a gun culture that does not exist in the rest of the civilized world. It has been estimated that there are now over 350 million guns in the United States, and the number increases with each passing year.

The New York Times printed a two-page spread on March 8, 2018, *What It Takes to Buy a Gun in 15 Countries*. It showed the United States at the top of the list, behind Yemen, as one of the easiest countries in which to purchase a gun. Those who prepared the list stated, "Many Americans can buy a gun in less than an hour. The process takes months in some countries."[6] Reports indicate that since 1970, an estimated 1.4 million Americans have died of gun violence, more than in all the wars in American history (1.3 million).[7] Statistics published in 2019 by Cable News Network (CNN), Turner Broadcasting System, Inc. and confirmed by the Center for Disease Control (CDC) show that 28,874 people died from gunshot wounds in the United States during 1999. That number increased to 39,773 by 2017.[8]

It began simply enough in 1607 with the original colonists. Driven by an urgent need to feed their families in the wilderness and to defend themselves and their property from wild animals and attacks by Native American tribes and foreign mercenaries, the colonists armed themselves. Firearms became essential in the daily struggle for food, freedom, and safety. Later they organized militias. The colonists didn't have any choice. The New World was a wild and dangerous place. It fostered a belief that gun ownership and carriage were unalienable rights.

During the French and Indian War, colonial militiamen picked up their muzzle-loaded, flintlock muskets as subjects of the English King and served beside British regulars. In that struggle over whether England or France would rule what is now the United States, a young lieutenant colonel, George Washington, led Virginia militiamen into battle at Great Meadows in western Pennsylvania in 1754. Washington lost that battle but later mustered colonists and their muskets into an army that drove out the British Redcoats during the Revolutionary War.

By the time George Washington resigned his military commission in 1783, a new nation had been born, and he had been named commander in chief of the United States Army.[9] When challenged again, the new nation called upon its citizen armies to fight and win the War of 1812. It is today a matter of immense national pride that firearms in the hands of dedicated patriots created the United States of America.

The demands placed on the colonists to defend themselves from foreign powers during these wars quite naturally solidified a reverence for private gun ownership that pervades our culture today. The overlapping roles that firearms played in colonial America equipped the colonists to serve in the Continental Army. A colonial minuteman knew how to fix the flint the hammer would strike, measure and pour black gun powder down the barrel of his muzzleloader, ram a bullet and wadding down the barrel with a ramrod, and then shoulder, aim, and fire his weapon. The roles that muskets played undoubtedly influenced the language describing the right to bear arms incorporated into the Second Amendment.

But we no longer live in colonial America. Military personnel today rigorously train to use their weapons and are subject to military discipline. Densely populated metropolitan regions occupy what was once wilderness. Now we have the FBI, National Guard units, state police, county sheriffs, and city police forces to protect society. Although the Constitution authorizes them, the necessity that patriots band together in organized militias to defend themselves no longer exists. As we shall see though, the provisions originally written into the Constitution for marshalling the militia into national service remain in place.

As the United States expanded westward, the Colt revolver, cartridges, and the repeating rifle were invented. Whatever the day-to-day life of those who travelled west in Conestoga wagons may have been, novelists and newspaper reporters romanticized the Wild West. They portrayed the pioneers who travelled west as cowboys who openly paraded the streets of cow towns with six-shooters strapped to their hips and rifles holstered on their horses. Gunslingers filed their weapons to create hair triggers so they could discharge their revolvers rapidly by fanning the hammer without pulling the trigger. Motion pictures and television idolized lawmen and criminals alike, including Wyatt Earp, Billy the Kid, and Jesse James. That romanticized history fortified a reverence for the American cowboy and for private gun ownership. Parents bought toy guns so that their children could emulate their comic book and movie idols in imaginary shootouts. Today digital video games are available to our children that portray acts of graphic gun violence.

Most new weaponry is inspired by war. The bloody battlefields of the Civil War exposed the need for soldiers with increased firepower. To meet that need deadlier weapons were introduced such as the tripod-mounted Gatling gun, the first firearm to solve the problems of loading reliability and firing sustained bursts. Experts didn't consider it a machine gun because it was hand driven, but it became the prototype for the machine guns fired on battlefields from the Spanish-American War onward. Those machine guns fed by belted ammunition were set pieces fired from tripods and clearly seen as military weapons. No one suggested, as far as is known, that set machine guns with belted ammunition were suitable for civilian use.

The Thompson submachine gun, also known as the tommy-gun and Chicago typewriter, was invented in 1918 by the American John J. Thompson. Held in the shooter's hands, it could fire over 600 rounds a minute and accommodate an extended drum magazine of 100 rounds. The tommy-gun reached its heyday during the Roaring Twenties. It was the weapon of choice for the 1929 Saint Valentine's Day Massacre in Chicago when Capone's gang shot up the Moran gang. They were romanticized on the silver screen in *The St. Valentine's Day Massacre, Bonnie and Clyde*, and the *Godfather* trilogy. What followed was a firestorm of deadlier firearms that flooded the markets and permeated our culture.

Mikhail Timofeyevich Kalashnikov, a Russian general and military engineer, invented the Kalashnikov automatic rifle at the close of World War II. That rifle fired with the accelerated speed of a machine gun. The shooter could discharge the rounds in its magazine while holding the weapon in his hands. The AK-47 and many knockoffs evolved from the Kalashnikov for armies and security forces all over the world. It has been estimated that 100 million AK-47s have been sold worldwide.[10] American mass shooters consider them a weapon of choice.[11]

The Constitution as originally drafted and ratified in 1787 did not set forth any right to own and carry firearms, nor did it prohibit them. The Bill of Rights, the first ten amendments to the Constitution, was drafted in New York by the first Congress of the United States—principally by James Madison—and ratified in 1791. The Bill of Rights included the Second Amendment, which provided: "A well regulated [sic] Militia, being necessary to the security of a Free State, the right of the people to keep and bear Arms, shall not be infringed."

The Second Amendment applied to Congress, but it did not originally apply to the states. The United States Supreme Court did not rule that the Second Amendment created a private constitutional right to own and carry firearms, separate from service in a state militia, for 220 years. The door was left open for federal and state governments to regulate firearms. Other provisions of the Bill of Rights seemed to support that conclusion.

The Ninth Amendment set forth in the Bill of Rights provided that, "The enumeration in the Constitution, of certain rights, shall not be construed to deny or disparage others retained by the people." The Tenth Amendment states: "The powers not delegated to the United States by the Constitution, nor prohibited by it to the States, are reserved to the States respectively, or to the people." That language appeared to support legislated gun regulation at the state and federal level, and the courts upheld that view.

But energized by the *Heller* and *McDonald* decisions, gun rights advocates now contend that their Second Amendment right covers a wide range of firearms and extends beyond the home into public venues. They are pushing nationwide for the right to open carry in public places.[12] Many states have enacted "stand your ground" laws that modify the common-law duty to retreat from a violent confrontation if one can do so safely and permit the use of deadly force in such a situation.[13]

The colonists' urgent need for firearms in our country's early years, the lucrative trade in firearms that developed from that need and political realities arising from the Second Amendment created and sustained today's culture of gun violence. Those whom the Supreme Court has labeled law-abiding gun owners, together with their legion of allies, assert that the Second Amendment is sacrosanct. Buried in the current debate is the fact that, while the Court held in *Heller* that *a municipal ban* on loaded handguns in the home was unconstitutional, it recognized (as we shall see) that Congress and the states can adopt reasonable laws and regulations for the sale, ownership, and carriage of firearms. Many gun rights people don't want to talk about the limitations on the right mentioned in *Heller.* They assert deep seated fears that limitations on the right to bear arms will lead to laws that take their guns away from them. Any new regulatory program for the private ownership and carriage of guns must recognize our history of gun ownership and deal with those deep-seated fears.

The gun debate also pits those living in rural areas against those living in our cities. Those who live in rural areas claim they need guns for self-defense because state police forces, local constables, and county sheriffs may be miles away when needed. They have a point. Yet, most of the tragic incidents described within these pages occurred in heavily populated urban areas where police forces are reasonably near at hand. Semiautomatic rifles, handguns, and extended magazines present an especially high risk in densely populated areas. Handguns are easily concealed and can be carried undetected into large crowds of people.

Modern technology permits home production of plastic firearms. Inexpensive 3-D printers can be purchased at local office supply stores. The internet has downloadable instructions on how to print a firearm that is difficult to detect with X-ray technology and metal detectors. The Undetectable Firearms Act of 1988[14] banned the manufacture, possession, and transport of firearms made with lightweight polymer components. That Act was renewed in 1998 and 2003 and later extended to 2023, but the National Rifle Association (NRA) opposed efforts to modernize or expand it.

Recently, the federal government approved a settlement of a lawsuit filed by Cody Wilson of Defense Distributed in which 3-D printing tutorials were approved for public release. The downloadable files reportedly include AR-15-style rifles similar to those used at Las Vegas, Newtown, Orlando, and Parkland. Mr. Wilson claimed a First Amendment right of free speech to distribute his tutorials and asserted that he is ushering in "the age of the downloadable gun." In a case that may end up in the United States Supreme Court, Judge Robert S. Lasnik of the United States District Court in Seattle entered a temporary nationwide injunction on August 27, 2018, to remain in effect until the case is resolved, blocking distribution of Mr. Wilson's tutorials.[15] Several other states joined the Seattle lawsuit. Other courts have issued similar rulings.[16]

Before *McDonald* was decided it was assumed that our states and local communities could regulate handguns to protect human life as part of their reserved police powers. Gang, school, workplace, suicide, and domestic violence present safety issues that have been seen historically as best handled at the local level. But state and local gun legislation lacks uniformity; it constantly changes and has failed to control gun violence. As a result of intense lobbying, our states and municipalities have not enacted laws that solved the problem and in many cases adopted ones that exacerbate the problem. The pistol grip shotgun-wielding gunman who wounded four police officers in a Detroit police station on January 23, 2011, drove the point home.[17] The shooter acquired his shotgun despite statutes enacted by the State of Michigan that made his acquisition and use of such a firearm a felony. The shotgun had been sold to a person with a felony conviction and later illegally sold or transferred to the shooter. Four fine police officers paid the price.

The private use of explosives and improvised explosive devices (IEDs), a by-product of our gun culture, is also a pressing national concern. During October 2018, 12 improvised bombs were mailed to Democrats. They didn't explode, but like the Murrah Federal Building bombing and 9-11, they tell us that today our lives are threatened by inadequately regulated firearms and explosives.

While the media gave wall-to-wall coverage to bloody massacres throughout 2018, Congress sat on its hands. Most candidates seeking national office in the 2018 mid-term elections rarely spoke about gun control or treated it as a hot issue. Like nothing that had happened really mattered. All the while gun dealers continued to routinely hawk semiautomatic firearms, extended magazines, bump stocks, and high velocity ammunition that some categorize as weapons of war. Unbelievable!

On November 5, 2018, one day before the general election, *Time* published a 26-page special report, "Guns in America", for which it created a dramatic three-page interactive cover of 245 photographic "voices" that cut through the silence. One of the persons interviewed stated, "The gun issue is the single most important issue facing America."

In an opinion piece appearing in *The New York Times* Gregory Gibson notes, "One hundred people die from the coronavirus and world freaks out. One hundred people are killed by guns each day in America and its business as usual. The ugly fact is that gun violence can happen wherever there are guns, and guns are everywhere: There are nearly 400 million civilian-owned guns in the country, and they're not going to go away." [18] It has been reported that the coronavirus pandemic that struck the United States in February and March of 2020 created a rush by first time buyers to purchase guns. Their motivation appears to be fear that the pandemic will produce lawlessness within the United States. One gun dealer saw his gun sales increase by 30 to 40 percent since late February 2020. [19]

Gun rights advocates are not only politicians and lobbyists. As a result of our history with guns and the resulting gun culture, thousands of our citizens fervently believe that they have an unalienable right to own and bear firearms for self-defense, hunting, and recreational use. They believe that guns are essential to protect themselves from the government and that the Second Amendment assures them of that right. Many of them assert we don't need more laws and that good guys with guns are the answer. These advocates may include one's family members, neighbors, and friends. They are *not* going to go away. But those who seek a more tranquil society and rational gun laws also include decent, law-abiding Americans who believe in the Constitution. They too include family members, friends, and neighbors.

Those who promote gun control have historically met strenuous opposition from those enamored of gun ownership. The voices touting gun ownership, through political action committees (PACs), advertising, and lobbyists have bottled up gun control at all levels. But we can no longer sweep the victims of gun violence at Parkland, Tree of Life, and El Paso along with all of the other victims of gun violence chronicled in this book, under the rug. America has to answer. It has to adopt a national policy of common sense gun control. In the words of Abraham Lincoln, it's time that we highly resolve that these dead shall not have died in vain.

Some on the gun-rights side of the debate seek to advance their position by referring to control side people as commies or socialists. The control side doesn't help matters when they label the other side gun nuts. Pejoratives will not tell us who our law-abiding citizens are. They will not define the weapons in common use at the time. Nor do they explain how the right to bear arms *Heller* created is limited. What is true is that *Heller*'s interpretation of the Second Amendment is now the law of the land.

The issue we face is whether and how the two views can be blended into a national policy that protects Second Amendment rights while bringing rampant gun violence under control. Neither side believes existing laws are adequate. Some say the answer lies in laws that identify the people who cannot safely own and carry firearms through background checks: felons, the mentally ill, and others unfit by temperament, age, etc. Others say the answer lies in laws that remove assault weapons, bump stocks, and extended loading devices from the general population. A new national policy on gun ownership and carriage can only happen if it respectfully accommodates the views of both groups. Representatives of both sides need to sit down at the same table, isolate areas of agreement, reach compromises where possible, and write a new paradigm. That is what our Founding Fathers did in Convention Hall in Philadelphia. That is what our gun problem needs now.

It is time to heed the message from the gun violence chronicled below.

CHAPTER 2

Our Constitution and Supreme Court Decisions to 2008

The right there specified is that of "bearing arms for a lawful purpose." This is not a right granted by the Constitution. Neither is it in any manner dependent upon that instrument for its existence.
— *United States v. Cruikshank*

G un violence arises not only from our history and the gun culture it developed. It is a by-product of our laws. The Constitution gave Congress powers that the Articles of Confederation lacked.[1] It proclaimed in its preamble that a new nation had been established to "form a more perfect union, establish justice, *insure domestic tranquility,* provide for the common defense, promote the general welfare, and secure the blessings of liberty to ourselves and our posterity." *Heller* is now the law of the land, but the constitutional debates, court cases, and statutes that preceded it are of critical importance. They give us background and help us understand what the Court did in *Heller* and what it did not do. Analysis of our gun problem must start with the constitution itself.

The world watched astounded as word went forth from Philadelphia that a new Constitution had been ratified by the original 13 states. Our Founding Fathers created a government never attempted before. Instead of a king or a dictator issuing decrees the new nation would be governed by its people through elected representatives and the rule of law. The nation our Constitution created is revered in song and poetry, and rightly so, but the survival of our nation under the rule of law has never been a given. Understanding the Second Amendment, its limitations, and exploring the source of Congressional and state power to regulate guns is now critical.

The vision of those who crafted our organic law* was that of a free people living in a republic where the legislative, executive, and judicial powers of the federal government were divided among three branches, where the powers of the federal government were separated from those of state and local governments, and where checks and balances built into the Constitution would protect against intrusion upon the life, liberty, and happiness of the people. When asked what form of government had been created Benjamin Franklin famously replied, "A republic if you can keep it."[2] Franklin's reply is as relevant today as it was when he uttered it.

The new government was not perfect. The issue of slavery threatened to destroy it. During the legislative battles that led to the Civil War, Abraham Lincoln described the federal government as "a house divided against itself."[3] Later at Gettysburg, Lincoln asked whether that new nation could long endure and expressed his concern and his hopes that government "of, by, and for the people shall not perish from the earth."[4] Lincoln understood that the powers granted by the Constitution were not self-executing, and that the answer to the question he asked at Gettysburg depended on whether the nation's elected representatives faithfully exercised the powers granted to them.

In Article I, Section 8, the Constitution granted Congress the power to tax and to regulate the manufacture, sale, ownership, and use of dangerous products sold in interstate commerce. Congress's Article I powers also include power to regulate commerce with foreign nations and among the states, to raise and support armies, to call forth the militia to "execute the laws" of the United States, and for arming and for governing such part of the militia employed in the service of the United States. In Section 8, Congress was also given power as necessary to execute its enumerated powers. Congress has ample designated and implied power to enact gun control if other parts of the Constitution do not forbid

---

*The body of laws (as in a constitution or charter) that form the original foundation of a government. Also, one of the laws that make up such a body.

it. The Constitution as originally ratified did not set forth an individual right to own and carry firearms nor did it prohibit them. Congress and state legislatures were not restricted by it from enacting gun controls. But did the Bill of Rights create a private right to bear arms outside of militia use?

Ratification of the first ten amendments to the Constitution—the Bill of Rights—concluded on December 15, 1791. It set forth freedoms that citizens of the United States would enjoy under the Constitution—freedom of speech, freedom of religion, freedom of the press, and freedom to publicly assemble—and restricted Congress from abridging or violating those freedoms. The Second Amendment provided: "A well regulated [*sic*] Militia, being necessary to the security of a free State, the right of the people to keep and bear Arms, shall not be infringed."

Shortly after the Constitution and the Bill of Rights were ratified, Chief Justice John Marshall stated in *Marbury v. Madison:* "The Government of the United States has been emphatically termed a government of laws and not of men."[5] That description of our constitutional government separates us from monarchies, oligarchies, and dictatorships. We rely on the rule of law. There is ample justification arising from the expansive interpretation of *judicial power* adopted in *Marbury vs. Madison* and in cases that followed it, however, to consider Chief Justice Marshall's description of our national government with skepticism. In that same opinion, Chief Justice Marshall also stated, "It is emphatically the province and duty of the Judicial Department to say what the law is."[6]

Much later another Chief Justice, Charles Evans Hughes, famously declared during a speech in Elmira, New York, on May 3, 1907: "We are under a Constitution, but the Constitution is what the judges say it is."[7] What then are the limits of that kind of judicial power? Consider that the Second Amendment was never amended through the legislative procedures provided in the Constitution. Were federal judges free to create a constitutional right to bear arms through the simple expedient of saying what the Second Amendment means?

For more than two centuries the Supreme Court did not interpret the Second Amendment as having created an individual right to own and carry firearms.[8] The opening words of the Second Amendment, "A well regulated [*sic*] Militia, being necessary to the security of a free State," were historically thought to qualify the "right of the people to keep and bear Arms . . . [that] shall not be infringed."

Under that interpretation the Second Amendment did not grant a right to keep and carry firearms independent from their use as part of a militia. The word *Arms* was written into the Second Amendment with a capital A and was believed to refer to military arms. Had James Madison and the first Congress of the United States, when drafting and ratifying the Amendment, intended to create a private right to keep and carry firearms apart from militia use, they could have simply said that the right to keep and carry firearms shall not be infringed without referring to the militia. They described other freedoms without using similar qualifiers.

To reach the result it later did in *District of Columbia v. Heller*[9] and *McDonald v. City of Chicago*,[10] the Supreme Court had to escape powerful precedent. In the famous *Slaughter-House Cases*,[11] an earlier Court had considered challenges to a Louisiana law permitting the creation of a state-sanctioned monopoly for butchering animals within the city of New Orleans. Justice Samuel Miller, who wrote the majority opinion in *Slaughter-House*, made a sharp distinction between rights derived from federal citizenship and those derived from state citizenship. He concluded that the privileges and immunities clause of the Fourteenth Amendment protected only those rights "which owe their existence to the Federal government, its National Character, its Constitution, or its laws."[12] Louisiana's state-sanctioned monopoly was not held to violate that clause. Four Justices (Field, Chief Justice Chase, Swayne, and Bradley) dissented.

The majority opinion in *Slaughter-House* expressed concern that if the privileges or immunities proposition advanced upon it was sound, "it would constitute this court a perpetual censor upon all legislation of the States, on the civil rights of their own citizens, with authority to nullify such as it did not approve as consistent with those rights, as they existed at the time of the adoption of this amendment."[13]

It had also been argued in *Slaughter-House* that the due process clause of the Fourteenth Amendment had been violated by the grant of a monopoly charter to the defendants. The Court made short shrift of that argument.

The first of these paragraphs (due process) has been in the Constitution since the adoption of the 5th amendment, as a restraint upon the federal power. It is also found in some form of expression in the constitutions of nearly all the States, as a restraint upon the power of the States. This law then, has been the same as it now is during the existence of the government except so far as the present amendment (The Fourteenth Amendment) may place the restraining power over the States in this matter in the hands of the Federal Government.

We are not without judicial interpretation, therefore, both state and national, of the meaning of this clause. And it is sufficient to say that under no construction of that provision that we have ever seen, or any that we deem admissible, can the restraint imposed by the State of Louisiana upon the exercise of their trade by the butchers of New Orleans be held to be a deprivation of property within the meaning of that provision.[14]

The Court's language in *Slaughter-House* was unusually strong. It held that neither the privileges and immunities clause, nor the due process clause of the Fourteenth Amendment gave it power to strike down the state statute before it there.

But *Slaughter-House* wasn't the whole story. Three years later the Supreme Court reviewed convictions that arose out of the infamous Colfax massacre in Louisiana on Easter Sunday 1873, where over one hundred blacks, many unarmed, were slaughtered by a band of armed white men. William Cruikshank and two others were convicted under the Enforcement Act of 1870[15] for banding and conspiring to deprive their victims of various constitutional rights, including the right to bear arms.

The Supreme Court held "the right to bear arms is not granted by the Constitution; neither is it in any manner dependent upon that instrument for its existence."[16] The *Cruikshank* Court said that, "The second amendment declares that [the right to bear arms for a lawful purpose] shall not be infringed; but this ... means no more than that it shall not be infringed by Congress."[17]

Later, in *Presser v. Illinois*,[18] which involved the rights of an unorganized militia, and again in *United States v. Miller*,[19] which dealt with the transportation of firearms in interstate commerce, the Court upheld its holding in *Cruikshank* that the Second Amendment applied only to the federal government.

Under the Supreme Court's interpretation of the Second Amendment that prevailed throughout the 19th and 20th centuries, no constitutional *private right* to bear arms apart from military use was ever declared. In 2008 (*Heller*) that approach was discarded.

CHAPTER 3

District of Columbia v. Heller

It is not the role of this Court to pronounce
the Second Amendment extinct.
—*Justice Antonin Scalia*

In a "dramatic upheaval of the law,"[1] the United States Supreme Court held five to four in *District of Columbia v. Heller* that the Second Amendment protects an individual's right to possess a firearm unconnected with service in a militia and to use that firearm for "traditionally lawful purposes, such as self-defense within the home."[2] Writing for the majority, Justice Scalia did not clarify what other uses are considered traditionally lawful. But he did allow that it was "not a right to keep and carry any weapon whatsoever in any manner whatsoever and for whatever purpose."[3]

The *Heller* opinion created enormous confusion for those seeking common sense gun regulations. The majority reached the result they did, they said, because the District of Columbia's ban on handgun possession in the home amounted to a complete prohibition of an entire class of arms that Americans overwhelmingly choose for the lawful purpose of self-defense.[4] The Court struck down requirements enacted by the District of Columbia that a handgun in the home be kept unloaded or disassembled, that it be kept in a lock box, or that it have a trigger lock. The *Heller* Court said that such requirements made it impossible to use the weapon for a "core lawful purpose of self-defense."[5] Critically though, the Court also said the District of Columbia's *licensing law* was "permissible so long as it is not enforced in an arbitrary and capricious manner."[6] That concession will be examined in a later chapter.

There are 27 words in the Second Amendment. Applying doctrines of textualism and original intent, Justice Scalia wrote 64 pages in *Heller* to parse that language and to tell us how the 14 words in the second clause of that Amendment created a private right to bear arms.

America will never achieve common sense gun control if it focuses only on the ruling in *Heller* that there is a private constitutional right to bear arms. The escalating events outlined below now demand that the limitations, qualifications, and exceptions to that right that Justice Scalia outlined in *Heller* be given muscle and sinew. It is therefore critical since we are dealing with the meaning of our organic law, to closely examine the precise holding of *Heller* as well as its *obiter dicta*, or incidental remarks. Even if *Heller* is seen as correctly decided, it left myriad cataclysmic questions unanswered and laid them aside for future decision.

Heller came down at a time when gun manufacturers, gun owners, and their lobbyists were clamoring for expanded rights to own and carry; more powerful weapons were coming on the scene; and the nation was reeling from the expiration of the assault weapon and extended magazine bans of 1994 and intensifying gun violence. The Court's opinion ignited a fierce struggle to expand the right to own and carry firearms that continues today. *Heller* needs rigorous analysis because gun rights advocates mouth the words *Second Amendment* as a shibboleth, or catch phrase, to cut off *all* gun regulation.

Political candidates hear: *There they go again; they're taking our guns away.* The Supreme Court's decision in *Citizens United v. Federal Election Commission,*[7] discussed below in Chapter 13, magnifies our politicians' concerns that if they do not support Second Amendment rights they will be "primaried" in August or outspent and defeated in November by the powerful gun rights lobby. Their concerns are not misplaced. If they don't fall in line, they may very well be defeated.

Heller is a most peculiar constitutional law decision. To begin with, as shown in Chapter 2, Justice Scalia was not writing on a clean slate when he penned the controlling opinion in *Heller*. An individual right to bear arms had never before been articulated by the Supreme Court as controlling constitutional law. It would have been better if the *Heller* Court had ruled more narrowly, left the Court's previous decisions undisturbed, and simply struck down the District of Columbia's ordinance[8] on the grounds it was a *complete ban on handguns* not disabled by a trigger lock or kept in a lock box.

The Court could have said the District's ban was an impermissible restriction on the right to own and carry arms even as part of a militia. The *Heller* Court, however, went *much* further. It saw an opportunity to establish a free-standing private right to own and carry firearms wholly separate from a right to carry them as part of a militia. It is difficult to understand why the Court chose in 2008 to sever the first phrase from the following clause of the Second Amendment and then proceed to articulate a private, limited constitutional right to own and carry firearms. Yet that is exactly what it did. In *Heller*, the Court confirmed what Chief Justice Charles Evans Hughes stated in Elmira, New York, a century before: the Constitution provides what the judges say it provides.

Who among us are the law-abiding citizens entitled to exercise the constitutional right to bear arms announced in *Heller*? Who among us can tell us who they are? How can a society dedicated to freedom and private enterprise keep weapons out of the hands of mass murderers, terrorists, and persons unfit to have them—while still protecting a law-abiding citizen's right to possess and bear firearms? Exactly where and how can they lawfully carry them?

The maddening, confusing issues created by *Heller* begin with its grammatical interpretation of the language in the Second Amendment. If the object of the Justices was to discern the Founding Fathers' original intent and lay it out there, how can the nation be certain what that intent was when only five Justices signed an opinion that laboriously attempted to say what it was, and four Justices dissented from their opinion?

Conservative members of the federal bench, as well as others, pontificate that the Constitution must be applied *as it was written*. When you drill down to specific words and phrases contained in the Constitution, that admonishment is difficult to apply. Interpretation involves choices. In the field of constitutional law, choice implicates the reach of judicial power. The Constitution did not vest the Supreme Court with a naked judicial power to create a private right to bear arms. If the Second Amendment as written did not set forth a private right to bear arms, the power to create such a right is legislative, exercisable by Congress or the states through statutory enactment or constitutional amendment. But the Second Amendment was never amended. It reads today as it did on the date it was ratified. The private right to bear arms the *Heller* majority found in the amendment came into being, if at all, upon its ratification in 1791, although no previous Court ever found it there.

Justice Scalia promoted textualism and originalism as interpretive tools. He used them to search for the meaning of words when they were written. In *Reading Law: The Interpretation of Legal Documents,*[9] Justice Scalia and coauthor Bryan A. Garner state: "The exclusive reliance on text when interpreting text is known as *textualism,*" but they acknowledge, "Words are to be given the meaning that proper grammar and usage would assign to them."[10]

These concepts are only two of the many the authors set forth to help find original intent. But how can we be sure what scriveners writing over 200 years ago meant if they intended something different than what they expressed in the words they chose? Where does one go to find their intent; whose original intent do we seek? Should it be that of the scrivener, the 26 senators and 65 representatives in the first Congress that ratified the Bill of Rights, legal scholars, contemporary writers, or that of the people? Do the normal rules of grammar apply? Was Chief Justice Charles Evan Hughes correct? Is original intent what today's Justices say it is?

In *Heller* Justice Scalia described the first 13 words of the Amendment as an introductory clause or a preface that did no more than announce a purpose. He said the prefatory clause did not limit the "operative clause" grammatically. That back in the day it was not unusual for sentences to contain prefaces or introductory clauses that stated the purpose of a sentence. The Northwest Ordinance of 1837, for example, provided that, "Religion, morality, and knowledge being necessary to good government and the happiness of mankind, schools and the means of education shall forever be encouraged." There the first phrase clearly states a specific reason why the Northwest Territories should establish the schools described in the following clause. A similar statement of purpose analysis for the Second Amendment would lead one to the conclusion that the right to bear "Arms" the Amendment described relates only to the stated purpose of maintaining a "well regulated militia." Indeed, that was Court's historic interpretation of the Amendment. But the Court in *Heller* refused to confine the Second Amendment right to bear arms to militia use.

Grammarians recommend that a sentence contain no unnecessary words.[11] The Amendment has one phrase and one clause. Grammatically, a clause is "a group of related words that contains a subject and a predicate, (verb)" and a phrase is "a group of related words that functions as a unit but lacks a subject or verb or both."[12] Whatever else it may be, the amendment is a single English sentence. The suggestion that sentences may contain introductory clauses or prefaces that state a purpose (here a right to bear arms as part of a militia) that does not in any way modify or limit words elsewhere expressed in the sentence is a novel one not found in grammar books. Nor has this author found the term *operative clause* in grammar books.

The introductory words—*a well regulated militia, being necessary to the security of a free State (sic)*—do not contain a predicate or an action verb. Under normal usage those words, whether a preface or not, are not a clause as stated by Justice Scalia. They are a phrase. Indeed, grammarians tell us they constitute an *adjectival modifier* or *adjective phrase*. The latter is defined as, "A word, phrase, or clause that acts as an adjective in qualifying the meaning of a noun or pronoun."[13]

To flesh that out further, grammarians define an adjective to be: "that part of speech that modifies a noun or other substantive by limiting, qualifying, or specifying and [is] distinguished in English morphologically by one of several suffixes such as -able, -ous, -or, -est, or *syntactically by position directly preceding a noun or a nominal phrase*."[14]

Under these definitions, the words "a well regulated Militia, being necessary to the security of a free State," are an adjectival modifier or adjective phrase that immediately precede and modify, limit, and qualify the nominal phrase, "the right of the people to bear Arms." To say otherwise destroys the sentence. There is no other noun or noun phrase contained in the Amendment that it could modify or limit. Whatever right to bear arms one may think should exist in the abstract, that is the way the Amendment was written by future president James Madison and the first Congress back in 1791. The right to bear arms contained in the Amendment was then, and it is now, grammatically qualified and limited on its face to be a right exercised by a well regulated militia. Otherwise, the first 13 words do not state a purpose; they have no work to do whatsoever. No use of firearms other than militia use is mentioned in the Amendment.

Even if the point is thought to be arguable, for more than 200 years no earlier Court found a private right to carry arms apart from well-regulated militia use in the Amendment. Justice Scalia looked to the English Bill of Rights, Sir William Blackstone's *Commentaries on the Laws of England*[*],[15] colonial constitutions, and so-called natural or inalienable rights to support a private right to bear arms for self-defense. Whether or not those authorities established such a private right, only the words written into the Amendment were before the Court. None of those sources are mentioned there.

The end result of Justice Scalia's lengthy explanation in *Heller* as to how it is that the Second Amendment provides a private right to bear arms outside of militia use is that the phrase and the clause contained in the amendment bear no relationship to each other whatsoever. Is that really what the Founding Fathers intended? According to *Heller*, the first phrase, "A well regulated [sic] Militia, being necessary to the security of a free State, [sic]," just floats out there in midair, having no relevance to the second clause or anything else. The first phrase, which states no private right to bear arms apart from militia use, becomes useless surplusage. Did the Founding Fathers intend to insert useless surplusage into the Constitution?

In his dissent in *Heller,* Justice Stevens strongly disagreed with the majority. For him the historical interpretation adopted in previous decisions was the most natural reading of the Amendment's text and "the most faithful to the history of its adoption." In an awesome expansion of judicial power, the majority in *Heller* rejected Stevens's views, laid aside the adjective phrase and held the "operative clause" created an ambiguous, not unlimited private right by law-abiding, responsible citizens to own and carry firearms in use at the time for lawful purposes at unspecified

---

*Sir William Blackstone (1723–1780) was a famous British Tory politician, jurist and educator who wrote *Commentaries on the Laws of England*, the first work since the 13th century to provide a comprehensive treatment of English law. His treatise discusses the rights of persons, the rights of things, of private wrongs and of public wrongs. The *Commentaries* played a role in the development of the American legal system.

places. In plain English the *Heller* Court did not read the Amendment as it was written. It struck some words and added others so it would read the way the Justices who signed the majority opinion wanted it to read.

Severe consequences flow from *Heller's* holding that the Second Amendment created a private right to bear arms. Many of them are discussed below. An example: According to news accounts a man in Florida recently accused a motorist of parking illegally. A member of the accused's family came on the scene and shoved the accuser to the ground. From a prone position the accuser drew a side arm and shot the unarmed attacker dead. Florida authorities refused to press homicide charges; reportedly on grounds the shooting was lawful under Florida's stand-your-ground law. Subsequent news reports said charges may be filed.

Two recent cases in the Ninth Circuit involved the right to carry a gun in public places. The first, *Peruta v. County of San Diego*[16] held that the Second Amendment right to keep and bear arms does not include "in any degree" the right of a member of the general public to carry concealed firearms in public. In the second, *Young v. Hawaii,*[17] the court, relying heavily on *Heller* and *MacDonald,* held that the Amendment does encompass a right to carry firearms openly in public for self-defense. These two cases demonstrate the confusion spawned by *Heller.*

Stand-your-ground combined with open carry threaten to take the nation back to the gun fight at the OK Corral, but now the participants would fire military assault weapons. Did the Justices in *Heller* intend to declare a constitutional right to openly carry firearms in public places where citizens would stand their ground as if in a matinée Western? What sort of criminal and civil liability will that create? What kinds of weapons—semi-automatics, large capacity magazines, bump stocks, hand grenades—may we carry? Would those policies apply to *all* public venues including the halls of Congress, the East Room of the White House, state legislatures, political gatherings, entertainment events, courthouses, places of worship, and schools? Would children, the blind, seniors, and the infirm be deemed physically and mentally capable of standing their ground in armed conflict? Would one state's policies apply in another state? What sort of nation do these policies create?

The Second Amendment could have provided simply that,

"The people's right to bear arms shall not be infringed," if that was the original intent. But then the language in the majority opinion in *Heller* describing the right to bear arms as a limited right would not fit. If the Founding Fathers intended to separate arms into two categories—military and civilian—where are the words in the Amendment that plainly say that? The first phrase certainly assumes that the possession of firearms and explosive devices by the militia should be well-regulated. But Justice Scalia's opinion tells us on its face that in the early days of the Republic the militia was a subset of the people. One could not well regulate the militia without well regulating the people who belonged to the militia. What then did the Amendment say about the rights of people not mustered into the militia? Should firearms they possess not be regulated at all? The dissent in *Heller* made a better argument when it said well-regulated relates to all uses of firearms.

The second clause, where Justice Scalia found a constitutional right to bear arms apart from militia use, states, "The right of the people to keep and bear Arms [*sic*], shall not be infringed." It does not employ *any* word or phrase that limits the right to bear arms announced in *Heller*. If, as Justice Scalia's opinion concedes, the constitutional right to bear arms is limited for reasons of safety, where do we find the words that spell out what those limitations are in the Second Amendment? Those words are simply not there. So where do they come from? Common sense dictates that you can't hand firearms to children, felons, terrorists, and the insane. The Founding Fathers could not possibly have intended that, and Justice Scalia's opinion recognized that fact, but the Court has no power to amend the Constitution, add words to it. Indeed, under Article V of the Constitution, amendment of the Constitution is exclusively a legislative function performed by Congress and state legislatures or conventions called for that purpose.

When Justice Scalia described the new right to own and carry firearms as a limited right and suggested several limitations on the right, he created more confusion. He wrote that prohibitions on concealed weapons would pass constitutional muster. He recognized that the Court's principal holding did not "cast doubt on longstanding prohibitions on the possession of firearms by felons and the mentally ill, on laws forbidding the carrying of firearms in sensitive places such as schools and government buildings, or on laws imposing conditions and qualifications on the commercial sale of arms."[18] As noted above, he also recognized that licensing laws are acceptable if not arbitrary or capricious. None of Justice Scalia's limitations, exceptions, or qualifiers can be found in the specific language contained in the Second Amendment unless they are encompassed by the phrase *well-regulated*. But you cannot find support there, because he split the Second Amendment in half and discarded the first phrase. His limitations, exceptions, and qualifiers, though quite rational and based on common sense, undercut the entire constitutional basis of the right to bear arms that he declared.

Having read the two clauses of the Second Amendment to segregate firearms according to their suitability for military or civilian uses, *Heller* didn't explain how to accomplish that segregation in the real world. Who should sort through and categorize the myriad weapons, along with all the parts that can be assembled into automatic weapons, now widely marketed and privately held? The Court said the right it pronounced applied to firearms, "in common use at the time," without clarifying what time period it was talking about. And how do we keep those two categories current with future technological changes?

In *Heller's* aftermath, the nation was left with the imperfect language of the Second Amendment, confusion over what *Heller* held, and a gargantuan gun problem. The regulatory difficulties created by *Heller* must be extracted from Justice Scalia's opinion and rigorously examined one by one.

Heller announced a constitutional right to keep and bear a functional, loaded handgun in one's home for self-defensive purposes, but it did not supply a means for identifying the law-abiding citizens to whom it said the right belonged. It did not delineate the specific firearms those law-abiding citizens could own or carry. It spoke about but did not restrict the places where law-abiding citizens could constitutionally carry firearms. It left broadly described limitations on the right for resolution in subsequent cases. After *Heller*, the District of Columbia and the rest of the nation would have to solve their problem with escalating handgun violence by filling in the blanks left by *Heller* through political means. Powerful political forces, however, have stalemated any effective gun regulation. Whatever else it may be, *Heller* was not a wise decision.

In *Heller,* Justice Scalia described the constitutional right to self-defense that he found in the Second Amendment to be a *not* un*limited right* that belonged to law-abiding citizens. But the people that he concluded have a private constitutional right to keep and carry firearms in their homes free of any regulation are also potential members of the militia that Congress can call forth, discipline, and *well-regulate* under other provisions of the Constitution that stand on their own apart from the Second Amendment.

The Second Amendment contemplated the existence of a well-regulated militia, and Article I of the Constitution gave Congress express powers to call forth the militia "to execute the laws of the Union, suppress insurrections, and repel Invasions." Congress was also given power for "organizing, arming, and *disciplining* the Militia."[19] (Chapters 11 and 12 will explore these powers below.) Under Justice Scalia's analysis, the so-called law-abiding citizen now wears two hats while he carries his weapons. Wearing one hat while defending himself in his home, he may not be regulated, but wearing the other hat while acting as militiaman and carrying the very same weapons, he may be well-regulated. How is that supposed to work?

The concept creates an image of persons who, having donned a law-abiding persona like a suit of armor, can be designated by a badge they wear or perhaps the color of their hats. It implies that a citizen's law-abiding status does not change as they travel from jurisdiction to jurisdiction. The concept presumes that there are rigid laws the law-abiding citizen can understand and abide by and that all agree on what those laws mean. But acts of violence like those described in the following pages reveal that a person's status as a law-abiding citizen may remain unknown until they pick up a weapon and kill someone. There is no statute or judicial decision that defines who the law-abiding are. The term seems to emanate from the advertising campaigns of the gun lobby which has used it to attack gun control for decades.

Justice Scalia's reference to arms "in common use at the time" is ambiguous at best.[20] It implies more than simply handguns kept in one's home for self-defense. To what period was he referring? From colonial times, Americans have used rifles and shotguns for hunting and recreation. That is not done inside the home. Weapons in general use at the time of the Revolution are described by Carl P. Russell's *Guns on the Early Frontier: From Colonial Times to the Years of the Western Fur Trade.*[21] Those weapons were single-shot firearms such as flintlocks and muskets loaded with a ramrod. Cartridges, clips, repeating rifles, and revolvers hadn't yet been invented. The *Illustrated Directory of 20th Century Guns* by David Miller[22] catalogs hundreds of modern automatic and semiautomatic weapons.[23] And with the range of guns and attachments so widely available on the gun markets today, the phrase *in common use at the time* is not a useful criterion to winnow out the specific guns that have constitutional protection. As new firearms are designed and manufactured, how can a gun dealer know which ones are weapons in common use at the time that he can sell to civilians coming into his store?

The weapons in Russell's and Miller's books are light-years apart. This is not to say that Justice Scalia meant to include only crude weapons of the type Russell describes, but the point is that Justice Scalia did not define in any useable manner the specific weapons that are protected under the Second Amendment. By indicating that machine guns, automatic weapons, assault weapons, and sawed-off shotguns were not protected,[24] Justice Scalia invited a more particular description. It is now up to Congress to supply that description.[25] In *Heller*, Justice Scalia seems to have conceded that the phrase *guns in common use at the time* does not include sawed-off shotguns, machine guns, or an M-16 rifle.[26] Earlier, a different Court said in *Miller*: "In the absence of any evidence tending to show that possession or use of a shotgun having a barrel of less than eighteen inches in length, at this time has some reasonable relationship to the preservation or efficiency of a well-regulated Militia, we cannot say that the Second Amendment guarantees the right to keep and bear such an instrument."[27]

When it wrote those words, the *Miller* court was clearly applying its understanding that the Second Amendment related only to the militia use of firearms. But the Court's refusal to apply the Second Amendment in *Miller*, Justice Scalia explained in *Heller*, was not based on "the defendants … bearing arms … for nonmilitary use" but that the "*type of weapon at issue* was not eligible for Second Amendment protection."[28]

Justice Scalia's interpretation of *Miller's* language is inconsistent with the result in *Miller*. That opinion held there was no private constitutional right to bear firearms. Justice Scalia used *Miller's* language in an effort to buttress his own interpretation of the Second Amendment, but in doing so he made a profound statement. His description of the underpinnings of *Miller* concedes that whole classes of firearms have no Second Amendment protection. It becomes legitimate to ask which weapons do have protection. Logic dictates that a modern semiautomatic rifle with an extended magazine is in the same category as a sawed-off shotgun or a fully automatic weapon. A Glock handgun with an extended magazine can fire 33 bullets in seconds from one clip and can be swiftly reloaded with a fresh clip.[29] After *Heller* how do such issues get decided?

Justice Scalia's opinion failed to provide a specific period one could employ to determine what weapons were in common use at the time. He didn't think it related only to the colonial period but did not declare what the intent of the Founding Fathers may have been. How could they have possibly formed an intent concerning weapons in common use at the time when they had no knowledge of the highly lethal, technologically superior weapons available today? It has even been suggested that the time period for determining what weapons were in common use at the time is a shifting standard, i.e., as the weapons favored by gun owners shift over time, the standard shall also shift, which does not fit with a constitutional right to bear arms.

Given the language of *Heller* though, determining what weapons were or are in common use at the time may now be a constitutional issue. Congress, the District of Columbia, and the states cannot legislate what weapons are in common use at the time. The issue of what weapons are included in the right can only be definitively resolved by a new Supreme Court opinion or a Constitutional amendment.

Given the lengthy, cumbersome appellate procedures of our courts, it is impractical to seek a case-by-case resolution to a host of critical questions the Court left open. The procedures for amending the Constitution require a two-thirds vote by both houses of Congress and a three-fourths vote by all state legislatures. That will not happen anytime soon in the existing political climate.[30]

Relying on the courts to tell us what weapons are in common use at the time is hazardous. After the Supreme Court decided Heller's first case, he filed another case in the Federal District Court for the District of Columbia. In the aftermath of *Heller,* the District had adopted a Firearms Control Regulation

Act amendment that required registration of firearms and prohibited registration of assault weapons and magazines with a capacity of more than ten rounds of ammunition, thus banning them. The District Court granted summary judgment in favor of the District upholding the new law.

Heller again appealed. The Second Circuit Court of Appeals affirmed the District Court in a two to one decision.[31] Judge (now Justice) Brett Kavanaugh's dissent, however, is highly relevant. Describing the AR-15 semiautomatic rifle as the "quintessential rifle that the District seeks to ban," Judge Kavanaugh would have struck down the District's ban because of his view that "the Second Amendment as construed in *Heller* [by the Supreme Court] protects weapons that *have not traditionally been banned and are in common use by law abiding citizens.*"

If Judge Kavanaugh considered the prodigious efforts of the gun lobby to prevent any legislated banning of firearms or the Congressional ban of semiautomatics that nevertheless was in effect from 1994 to 2004, he gave no weight to either. Under Judge Kavanaugh's interpretation of *Heller* (should that interpretation ever become the law of the land) AR-15 semiautomatic rifles currently being used for mass murder along with who knows what other firearms—bazookas, 3-D printed guns?—become constitutionally protected firearms by popular choice and cannot be banned by legislated law. That is not the rule of law. It is a race to the bottom to mob rule. Should Justice Kavanaugh's interpretation be adopted, in the future even weapons not yet invented could be held to be weapons "in use at the time" that are protected by the Amendment. In all due respect to Justice Kavanaugh, recent polls reveal that the vast majority of Americans want semi-automatic firearms removed from civilian life.

The Supreme Court's decision in *Heller* did not explain how any regulation could reduce gun violence where the utility of any given firearm is not restricted to a Second Amendment right of self-defense in the home, and no regulatory structure currently exists to effectively separate military-style assault weapons from legitimate self-defense weapons. Handguns of the type at issue in *Heller* and *McDonald* are readily transported far outside the home. Semiautomatic firearms can be equipped with extended magazines and even converted to be fully automatic. Moreover, establishing a right to keep and carry an assembled, loaded handgun in the home by law-abiding citizens does not ensure that felons, the mentally deranged, or minors who may live in the home of such a protected person or visit there, have no access. Nor does it prevent the weapon from being used outside the home for other purposes, including mass murder, school shootings, terrorism, and so-called private militia purposes that are not well-regulated.

The Court's opinion in *Heller* has been vigorously criticized. Robert W. Ludwig, a Washington, D.C. attorney and counsel to the American Enlightenment Project, wrote: "The effects of Heller are devastating. Since it opened the floodgates, there have been three hundred thousand deaths and counting, another every fifteen minutes, with millions wounded physically or psychologically, already half the Civil War carnage sparked by *Dred Scott v. Sandford*."[32] Ludwig argues that the Second Amendment's full text, usages, and history were never presented or addressed in *Heller*, and that it should receive "a proper burial."

In his book, *Tyranny of Words*,[33] Stewart Chase analyzed the power of words. Chase explained how words mean different things to different people and the difficulty of extracting meaning from them. The Cook Quadrangle at the University of Michigan Law School has etched into its stone walls: *The life of the law has not been logic, it has been experience.*[34] Those terse words tell us that justice does not come from the application of words alone. We also need the wisdom of experience.

While *Heller* and later *McDonald* left the door open for more regulation, among the issues *Heller* didn't resolve are:

- Identification of the law-abiding, responsible citizens who are entitled to exercise the right
- Description of the lawful uses to which the right applies
- Definition of the specific firearms that have constitutional protection
- Clarification of whether weapons may be carried openly or concealed
- Elaboration of the extent to which the new constitutional right extends beyond the home and out into public places
- Adequacy of our licensing laws

After *Heller* where do we go to get an explanation of the exceptions to the right described in *Heller* and resolve these issues? Currently, Congress and the gun lobby won't even let us ask that question. Recall also, that *Heller* only involved the power of the federal government to enact gun regulations. Did the ruling in *Heller* apply to gun regulation by the states? That answer came two years later in *McDonald*.

CHAPTER 4

McDonald v. City of Chicago

The due process clause of the Fourteenth Amendment incorporates the Second Amendment right [to bear arms].
— *Justice Samuel Alito*

The right to keep and bear arms is a privilege of American citizenship that applies to the States through the Fourteenth Amendment's privileges or immunities clause.
— *Justice Clarence Thomas*

The dividing line between Congressional power and the powers reserved to the states has been elusive and shifting. After Article 1 Section 8 granted Congress certain enumerated powers, the Tenth Amendment provided: "The powers not delegated to the United States by the Constitution, nor prohibited by it to the States, are reserved to the States respectively or to the people." Police power has been exercised by the states since the inception of our nation, but what are its limits?

The Court's *Heller* decision exponentially magnified the handgun problem our cities, their residents, and their police forces faced. But *Heller* only dealt with the power of the federal government to restrict the right to have and carry a handgun in the District of Columbia, a federal enclave controlled by Congress. That left, at the least, an inference that under the Tenth Amendment, a state law that banned a handgun in the home or elsewhere would pass muster. The Second Amendment had never been held to be binding on the states. Historically, state legislatures and municipalities exercised their Tenth Amendment police powers to enact laws to control handguns. As soon as *Heller* struck down the District of Columbia ban, gun rights advocates immediately looked for an opportunity to ask the Court to strike down state regulation that interfered with the new federal constitutional right announced in *Heller*.

To meet the crisis in public health and safety which firearms posed and relying on their police powers, Chicago and the neighboring city of Oak Park had adopted handgun control ordinances much like the one adopted by the District of Columbia. Chicago's ordinance[1] essentially banned the possession of all handguns in the homes of private citizens in Chicago. The Oak Park ordinance was similar.

A federal Second Amendment right to bear arms in the home or otherwise, if it applied to Illinois and the cities of Chicago and Oak Park, would trump classic state police power. In 2010, while constitutional experts and political pundits were still discussing the ramifications of the *Heller* decision, the Court in *McDonald* extended its holding in *Heller* to the states. A plurality of Supreme Court Justices ruled in *McDonald* that the Second Amendment right articulated in *Heller* was binding on the states under the Fourteenth Amendment, but the plurality disagreed on which clause of the Fourteenth Amendment required that result. Nevertheless, the Court's ruling meant that Chicago's and Oak Park's attempts to ban handguns in the home were dead in the water, as was any similar state statute or municipal ordinance.

The due process clause of the Fourteenth Amendment reads: "Nor shall any state deprive any person of life, liberty, or property, without due process of law." This wording is markedly different than its privileges and immunities clause which reads: "No state shall make or enforce any law which shall abridge the privileges or immunities of citizens of the United States."

In one the states shall not deprive, whereas in the other the states shall not make or enforce any law. In one, the protected right is life, liberty, or property; in the other the right is a privilege or immunity of citizens of the United States. Yet the Court's decision in *McDonald* spread the Court's ruling in *Heller* over all the states.

When critically examined, *McDonald* is weak precedent. Almost as soon as *Heller* came down, petitioners including the NRA asked the Supreme Court to apply the *Heller* decision to the City of Chicago and the City of Oak Park, Illinois, on the grounds their gun ordinances were the same as the District of Columbia hand-gun ban struck down in *Heller*. But there had been little seasoning of *Heller* in the federal courts or in academia before the Court was asked to apply the same restriction on Congress's power to regu-late guns to the reserved police power of the states.

The issue presented in *McDonald* lacked clarity because the petitioner gun owners argued that the bans adopted by Chicago and Oak Park violated their right to keep and bear arms, primar-ily because that right was a privilege or immunity accorded them under the Fourteenth Amendment and secondarily because the Fourteenth Amendment's due process clause incorporates the Second Amendment right.[2] Those two concepts are set out as separate and distinct restrictions on the states in the Fourteenth Amendment, and the Court has traditionally applied them that way. Further, the Court traditionally did not invoke the privileges and immunities clause to incorporate Bill of Rights guarantees against the states.

Whatever ambiguity there may have been in petitioners' briefs, Justice Alito's opinion in *McDonald* interpreted the appeal of the Chicago and Oak Park handgun bans as squarely present-ing the question whether the Second Amendment restricted only Congress. The Court had never before held that any rights set forth in the Second Amendment restricted the states under either the privileges and immunities clause or the due process clause of the Fourteenth Amendment.[3] To reach the result it did in *McDon-ald*, the Court had to find a way to reverse or otherwise explain away the *Slaughter-House* cases[4] and cases following *Slaughter-House* like *Cruikshank*, *Presser*, and *Miller*, which held that neither the due process clause nor the privileges and immunities clause could be used to restrict the power of the states to regulate guns.

As a matter of tradition, if not *stare decisis*, the Supreme Court shies away from reversing settled precedent and from find-ing new Constitutional rights that deprive Congress or the states of their reserved powers. Justice Samuel Alito acknowledged that aspect of Supreme Court jurisprudence in *McDonald,* but then he cited the *amici curiae** filed by constitutional law professors that

---

*Latin phrase that means "friend of the court." (Pl. *amici curiae*) A person or group who is not a party but has accepted expertise or insight on the issues in the case, will petition the court for permission to submit a brief in the action with the intent of influencing the court's decision.

stated the "overwhelming consensus among leading constitutional scholars" was that the *Slaughter-House* opinion was "egregiously wrong."[5] *Slaughter-House* was headed for the dust bin as far as the Second Amendment was concerned.

The Fourteenth Amendment, ratified on July 9, 1868, provided in part that no state shall "deprive any person of life, liberty, or property without due process of law." Later, in a number of criminal cases, the Supreme Court began to incorporate many of the rights set forth in the Bill of Rights—which was originally construed to be binding only on Congress and not on the states—into the due process of law guarantee contained in the Fourteenth Amendment, and to enforce them against the states in state criminal proceedings. The right to trial by jury,[6] the right to defense counsel,[7] and the right not to testify against oneself[8] to name three were incorporated into the due process guarantee of the Fourteenth Amendment. Then in later cases, the Court began to enforce other rights it drew from the Bill of Rights against the states that were not procedural in nature, such as the right of privacy,[9] by incorporating them through the due process clause of the Fourteenth Amendment. That type of incorporation became known as *substantive due process*. Justice Alito extensively reviewed that history in his opinion in *McDonald*.[10]

But the law denying application of the Second Amendment to the states through the Fourteenth Amendment remained in the posture laid out in the *Cruikshank* line of cases until the Court's decision in *McDonald*. There, four justices—Alito, Chief Justice Roberts, Scalia, and Kennedy—did what the Court had said it would not do in *Cruikshank, Presser,* and *Miller.* They said that "the Fourteenth Amendment's due process clause incorporates the Second Amendment right recognized in *Heller*."[11]

Before *McDonald* was decided it had been settled for over a century that the due process clause of the Fourteenth Amendment applies to matters of substantive law as well as matters of procedure. Plainly, if the Second Amendment is construed to provide a private constitutional right to bear arms, that guarantee is substantive, not procedural. Justice Alito's opinion recognized that, and Justice Stevens pointed it out in dissent.[12]

However, Justice Thomas in his separate concurrence in *McDonald,* while agreeing that the Second Amendment right to bear arms was fundamental to the American "scheme of ordered liberty" and "deeply rooted in the nation's history and tradition," stated: "I cannot agree that it is enforceable against the States through a clause that speaks only to process."[13] Justice Thomas went on to declare that "*Cruikshank* is not a precedent entitled to any respect.... Instead, the right to keep and bear arms is a privilege of American citizenship that applies to the States through the Fourteenth Amendment's privileges or immunities clause."[14]

Thus, while five justices agreed in *McDonald* that the Fourteenth Amendment incorporated a Second Amendment substantive right to keep and bear arms, only four grounded incorporation on the due process clause, while the fifth expressly rejected that clause and rested incorporation on the privileges and immunities clause, which the other four in the plurality had expressly rejected. There is no majority opinion in *McDonald* in which five Justices joined unless: (1) the opinions can be read such that Justice Thomas, while he did not agree the Fourteenth Amendment's due process clause could be used, nevertheless signed on to a judgment that held it did, or (2) the Fourteenth Amendment incorporates the Second Amendment either under the due process clause or under the privileges and immunities clause. President Lincoln told us: "A house divided against its self cannot stand." Neither should a Supreme Court opinion. It was as if the Court believed the house President Lincoln spoke of could stand on two wholly separate foundations drawn from the Fourteenth Amendment.

An either/or analysis is strained. So far as known, no previous Fourteenth Amendment case incorporated provisions of the Bill of Rights to restrict a state's police power on an either/or analysis. Justice Alito categorically stated in his opinion in *McDonald*: "We see no need to reconsider [*Slaughter-House*] here. For many decades, the question of which rights are protected by the Fourteenth Amendment against state infringement has been analyzed under the due process clause of that Amendment and not under the privileges or immunities clause. We therefore decline to disturb the *Slaughter-House* holding."[15]

But if *McDonald* did not reverse it, then *Slaughter-House* is still good law, as are the cases that followed it. In *Slaughter-House*, the Court had expressly rejected the privileges and immunities clause of the Fourteenth Amendment stating it only applied to privileges and immunities of citizens of the United States:

"It is quite clear, then, that there is a citizenship of the United

States, and a citizenship of a state, which are distinct from each other, and which depend upon different characteristics or circumstances in the individual ... the next paragraph of this same section ... speaks only of privileges and immunities of citizens of the United States."[16]

But, adamant in his concurrence in *McDonald*, Justice Thomas wrote that the privileges and immunities clause and *not* the due process clause should be used to incorporate the Second Amendment against the states:

> But any serious argument over the scope of the due process clause must acknowledge that neither its text nor its history suggests that it protects the many substantive rights this Court's cases now claim it does. . . . I believe the original meaning of the Fourteenth Amendment offers a superior alternative, and that return to that meaning would allow this Court to enforce the rights the Fourteenth Amendment is designed to protect with greater clarity and predictability than the substantive due process framework has so far managed.[17]

> Three years after *Slaughter-House*, the Court in *Cruikshank* squarely held that the right to keep and bear arms was not a privilege of American citizenship, thereby overturning the convictions of Militia members responsible for the brutal Colfax Massacre. . . . *Cruikshank* is not a precedent entitled to any respect. The flaws in its interpretation of the privileges and immunities clause are made evident by the preceding evidence of its original meaning, and I would reject the holding on that basis alone.[18] . . . *I agree with the Court that the Second Amendment is fully applicable to the States. I do so because the right to keep and bear arms is guaranteed by the Fourteenth Amendment as a privilege of American citizenship.*[19]

Justice Thomas's interpretation may be correct, but not one of the other Justices agreed with him on the application of the Fourteenth Amendment. It cannot be said that a majority of the *McDonald* Court held that either the due process clause or the privileges and immunities clause of the Fourteenth Amendment incorporates the Second Amendment. Justice Thomas acting alone could not reverse *Cruikshank* or the cases that followed it. The result is that *Heller* applies to the states, but on what theory? Should future cases be analyzed as due process cases or privileges and immunities cases? There are major differences between the two clauses. If the right is a privilege of United States citizens, the states are left with little or no wiggle room and a single national standard would apply. Yet, like *Heller, MacDonald* is now the law of the land.

No definitive studies have been found to tell us whether *Heller* and *MacDonald* led to an increase in gun violence, but statistics and news reports of gun violence are escalating. A better question is whether those decisions have crippled legislative power and frustrated the enactment of new laws. Some states, New York and California in particular, have enacted red flag laws and laws to expand background checks and to ban semiautomatics and extended loading devices. But not all have. Scalia stated in *Heller* that the new constitutional right did not prevent Congress from banning guns in "sensitive places such as schools and government buildings." The recent attempt to legislate open carry in Michigan schools (described below in Chapter 5) demonstrates that the states are either unable to ban the carriage of firearms in their schools or they won't. The decisions in *Heller* and *McDonald* invite Congressional action. But since the national semiautomatic ban expired in 2004, there has been a near total collapse of legislative efforts at both the state and national levels. The next chapter examines our existing gun laws and reveals that except for some laws in some states *Heller's* limitations, qualifications, and exceptions have not been enacted into law.

CHAPTER 5

Existing Federal and State Statutes

The arms are fair, when the intent of
bearing them is just.
— *Shakespeare, HENRY IV*

The history of regulating semiautomatic assault weapons and extended loading devices like those used at Las Vegas, Stoneman Douglas, El Paso, and Dayton exemplify the contortions Congress performs to avoid enacting effective laws controlling what many see as military assault weapons. The laws we now have reveal those contortions.

A. Machine guns, silencers, and sawed-off shotguns

It began with the National Firearms Act of 1934.[1] That Act (NFA) did not set fixed standards to regulate firearms, nor did it ban machine guns or sawed-off shotguns. It imposed a tax on "a shotgun or rifle having a barrel of less than eighteen inches in length, or any other weapon, except a pistol or revolver, from which a shot is discharged by an explosive if such weapon is capable of being concealed on the person, *or a machine gun*, and includes a muffler or silencer for any firearm whether or not such firearm is included within the foregoing definition." [2]

Under the 1934 Act, private gun owners could keep the firearms they had and buy more if they obtained approval from the Bureau of Alcohol, Tobacco, and Firearms (ATF), passed a background check, registered their NFA firearm with the ATF, and paid the tax. The law also required that importers, manufacturers, and dealers of NFA firearms be licensed. If an individual owner of an NFA weapon wished to sell or transfer it, the new owner had to reregister the weapon in their name with the NFA registry.[3]

The 1934 Act allowed prosecutors to use information supplied to the ATF by people registering their firearms as evidence in criminal trials, but in 1968 the Supreme Court ruled 7–1 in *Haynes v. U.S.* that the use of such information violated an individual applicant's right against self-incrimination.[4] Some thought that ruling had the effect of nullifying the 1934 Act, although only part of the Act was held to be unconstitutional.

Today, it is still lawful to own registered machine guns originally acquired before May 19, 1968—the date the Gun Control Act of 1968 took effect. They are currently sold and transferred at many times their original value. The 1968 Act, however, changed the law from a firearms tax to a machine gun ban. It stated: "It shall be unlawful for any person other than a licensed importer, licensed manufacturer, or licensed dealer *to transport in interstate or foreign commerce* any destructive device, machine gun (as defined in section 5848 of the Internal Revenue Code of 1954), short-barreled shotgun, or short-barreled rifle, except as specifically authorized by the Secretary." [5] That provision is still in effect.

B. Semiautomatic pistols and rifles and high capacity magazines

The 1968 Act banned machine guns acquired after that act took effect, but did not ban semiautomatic rifles or pistols or high capacity magazines. That changed when Congress enacted the Violent Crime Control and Law Enforcement Act of 1994,[6] which stated, "It shall be unlawful for a person to manufacture, transfer, or possess a semiautomatic assault weapon."[7] The 1994 Act distinguished a semiautomatic firearm that "requires a separate pull of the trigger to fire each cartridge,"[8] from a machine gun which fires multiple rounds by "a single function of the trigger."[9] Using that definition, the firearms outlawed by the 1994 Act included Avtomat Kalashnikovs, UZIs, Beretta Ar70s, and Colt AR-15s. That Act also defined semiautomatic assault weapons by referring to the type of stock (folding or telescoping), bayonet mounts, flash suppressors, grenade launchers, and detachable magazines. The 1994 Act did not apply to any semiautomatic assault weapon "that cannot accept a detachable magazine that holds more than five rounds of ammunition or ... more than five rounds in a fixed or detachable magazine."[10]

Although it was a milestone ban on the private use of some semiautomatic military assault firearms and high capacity magazines, the 1994 Act contained numerous qualifications and exceptions. For openers, the 1994 ban did not apply to "any semiautomatic assault weapon lawfully possessed under Federal law on the date of enactment of this sub-section."[11] Nor did it apply to "any of the firearms … specified in Appendix A to the Act, if those firearms "were manufactured on October 1, 1993."[12] Appendix A,[13] printed right in the Act itself, listed approximately 630 firearms by manufacturer name and model number that were excluded from the definition of a banned semiautomatic firearm. When you examine the exceptions to the 1994 Act you see the fine hand of the lobbyists at work. Still, it did ban some military assault semiautomatics, at least up to a point.

The 1994 Act also made it unlawful to sell or own a large-capacity ammunition feeding device—defined as "a magazine … or similar device that has a capacity of or can be … converted to accept more than ten rounds of ammunition"[14]—unless it had been owned on or before the date the act went into effect on September 13, 1994.

Not only did the hundreds of exceptions written into the 1994 Act weaken its effort to regulate semiautomatic firearms, but so did its sunset provisions. Section 110105 of the 1994 Act repealed the semiautomatic assault weapon provisions it contained after ten years—September 13, 2004—unless Congress extended the Act.[15] It did not. The 1968 Act (current federal law)[16] still makes it unlawful for licensed importers, manufacturers, dealers, and collectors to transport, sell, or deliver any "destructive device"—including machine guns, short-barreled shotguns, short-barreled rifles, or armor piercing ammunition, but as of September 13, 2004, federal law no longer banned semiautomatic assault weapons and high capacity magazines.

Those who transferred the high capacity drum magazine, 6,000 rounds of ammunition and the AR-15 semiautomatic assault rifle to the Aurora shooter in 2012[17] (discussed in Chapter 8 below) would have committed felonies under the 1994 Act, except that Act expired in 2004. The AR-15s later used in massacres at Sandy Hook, Stoneman Douglas, and other venues were specifically designated as illegal weapons in the expired 1994 Act because they accepted detachable magazines that held more than five rounds.

C. Semiautomatics equipped with an extended loading device

It's sensible to ask whether a semiautomatic assault rifle fitted with an extended loading device and a bump stock is in fact legal under current federal law. But the language in the federal statutes is far from clear. The National Firearms Act of 1934, the seminal statute for federal gun control, did not make it a felony to possess a machine gun as defined in that Act. It imposed a tax on them and required that they be registered.

When Congress enacted the Gun Control Act of 1968 it sought to resolve the self-incrimination issue decided by the Supreme Court in *Haynes v. U.S.* and rewrote the 1934 Act. As we've seen, Section 922(a)(4) of the 1968 Act made it unlawful for any person to transfer or possess a machine gun or short-barreled shotgun,[18] but it exempted military personnel and police, and machine guns and sawed-off shotguns lawfully transferred or possessed prior to the 1968 Act's taking effect.[19] That left a substantial number of unregulated machine guns and sawed-off shotguns still possessed by the civilian population.

Critically, the 1968 Act defined a machine gun as any weapon that automatically shoots more than one shot by a single function of the trigger. "The term shall also include the frame or receiver of any such weapon, any part designed and intended solely and exclusively, or combination of parts designed and intended, for use in converting a weapon into a machine gun, and any combination of parts from which a machine gun can be assembled if such parts are in the possession or under the control of a person."[20]

That language would not ban a semiautomatic rifle because semiautomatics require separate trigger pulls for each shot. But trigger activators and bump stocks that came on line in the late 20th century accelerated the firing rate of a semiautomatic rifle to emulate that of a machine gun. Even though the 1994 Act banning semiautomatics had expired, it is possible to argue that the semiautomatics used at the Mandalay massacre in Las Vegas (described in Chapter 7), when equipped with bump stocks and extended loading devices, were unlawful machine guns under the definitions of the 1968 Act.

The Slide Fire bump stock (discussed below) when attached to an AR-15 appears to be a "part designed and intended solely and exclusively" to convert a firearm into a machine gun prohibited by the 1968 Act. Similarly, a semiautomatic rifle, bump stock, and expanded magazine (like those used at the Mandalay Bay in Las Vegas) appear to be a combination of parts "from which a machine gun can be assembled if such parts are in the possession of or under the control of a person." If these interpretations are held to be true, then the transfer, and certainly the possession of the semiautomatics, bump stocks, and accelerated loading devices used at Mandalay Bay, were felonies under the 1968 Act—except, as we shall see, John Spencer, the ATF's chief of firearms technology had ruled in 2010 that the Slide Fire bump stock was not a firearm.[21] It would make more sense if the law defined a machine gun and a semiautomatic weapon (whether as originally manufactured or later altered) according to the highest potential rate at which the firearm can discharge rounds through its barrel.

In *Staples v. United States*,[22] the Supreme Court said:

> As used here, the terms "automatic" and "fully automatic" refer to a weapon that fires repeatedly with a single pull of the trigger. That is, once the trigger is depressed, the weapon will automatically continue to fire until its trigger is released or the ammunition is exhausted. Such weapons are "machineguns" within the meaning of the Act. We use the term "semiautomatic" to designate a weapon that fires only one shot with each pull of the trigger, and which requires no manual manipulation by the operator to place another round in the chamber after each round is fired.

The Court was using the definition used in the Gun Control Act of 1968. The term *trigger* was not defined in that Act. In *United States v. Jokel*,[23] which pertained to a shotgun, the Court defined a trigger for purposes of 26 USC Section 5845(d) as any "mechanism ... used to initiate the firing sequence." That definition was approved in *United States v. Fleischli*,[24] which did concern a machine gun. In *United States v. Evans*,[25] also a machine-gun case, the Ninth Circuit defined a trigger as "anything that releases the bolt to cause ... [the weapon] to fire."

In *United States v. Camp*,[26] the defendant had rigged a switch behind the original trigger that supplied power to an electric motor that rotated a reel placed behind the trigger guard. The rotation of the reel caused the weapon to fire in rapid succession until either the shooter released the switch or the ammunition was expended. Camp argued the device was merely a *trigger activator*, and that the weapon was not a machine gun. On appeal, the Fifth Circuit considered a District Court order that had dismissed Camp's indictment on grounds his weapon was not a machine gun. The Fifth Circuit reversed, cited the above cases, and determined Camp's weapon was in fact a machine gun. "Camp's weapon, however, required only one action—pulling the switch he installed—to fire multiple shots. This distinction is expressly contemplated by Sec. 5845 (b), which speaks of 'shooting automatically more than one shot ... by a single function of the trigger.'"[27] But does the *Camp* opinion apply to bump stocks?

D. The bump stock story

Okay, the semiautomatic weapons ban expired in 2004; that's a fact. But the ingenuity and perseverance of persons addicted to innovative gun design, manufacture, and ownership didn't expire. Their drive for ever greater firepower produced the bump stocks found in Stephen Paddock's Mandalay Bay hotel suite in Las Vegas, along with trigger activators and other devices designed to accelerate the firing rate of a semiautomatic rifle. It is critical to understand the bump stock story because it reveals the havoc that unregulated altered weapons can produce.

William Atkins invented one version of the bump stock and marketed it through his company, Bump Fire Systems. Atkins filed for a patent on his bump stock and obtained US Patent No. 6,101,918 for the device on August 15, 2000. Recall that under the 1994 Act semiautomatics sold prior to the effective date of that Act were lawful firearms that were excepted from the Act and are still possessed by civilians. So there was a market for Atkins's invention and an even greater one if Congress let the 1994 assault weapons ban expire.

At the time Atkins applied for and received his patent, machine guns together with semiautomatic rifles and pistols transferred or first possessed after the 1994 Act took effect were illegal. Yet the claims Atkins made for his patent (you have to read the patent) revealed he had deliberately designed and patented his bump stocks so that his bump stock would, "accelerate the cyclic firing rate of a semiautomatic firearm."[28] If true it allowed the conversion of a legal semiautomatic rifle to one that likely violated federal law at that time. When attached to a semiautomatic it permitted the gun's original stock and trigger to move back and forth in a sliding device Atkins placed in the bump stock, described in the legalese of his patent attorneys as an "accelerating mechanism that incorporates structure that permits the receiver *and trigger* to translate rearwardly a predetermined distance."

When firing a semiautomatic with a bump stock attached, a shooter would hold the semiautomatic in his two hands and loosely against his shoulder. When he fired the first round the recoil of the weapon drove it back against his shoulder and the trigger reset. Continuous forward pressure applied throughout the shooting cycle by his non-trigger-finger hand slid the weapon back to its original position bringing the trigger of the weapon back into contact with his stationary trigger finger, thereby discharging the next round to continue the shooting cycle.

Atkins's patent expressly stated that after initiating the shooting cycle, the shooter's trigger finger remained stationary and was held in position by a "locating stop" device Atkins designed into the bump stock. Atkins's bump stock permitted a semiautomatic rifle to fire at a rate like that of a fully automatic weapon—between 400 and 600 rounds per minute.[29] His device would fire a semiautomatic faster than a shooter could pull the trigger. Atkins's patent claims stated:

> When one understands the operational distinction between automatic and semiautomatic firearms, it can be readily understood that the CYCLIC FIRING RATE for a semiautomatic FIREARM is normally limited by the reaction time within which the shooter can squeeze the trigger to fire a round, release the trigger as the FIREARM recoils in response to discharge of the first round, and then re-squeeze the trigger to discharge the next successive round. Although the cyclic time will differ from shooter to shooter, even the most practiced shooter will be unable to discharge more than two or three rounds at a rate less than about one round per second.

Atkins's patent went on to claim: "It is, therefore, a primary object of the present invention to provide an improved method and apparatus by which the cyclic firing rate of a semiautomatic firearm can be selectively accelerated."

The ATF did not approve the Atkins's version of the bump stock after evaluating it, ostensibly because it utilized springs to return the receiver and trigger back to the starting position.

The bump stock story did not end with the rejection of the Atkins's patent by the ATF. Jeremiah Cottle obtained US Patent No. 8,127,658 on March 6, 2012, for: "A method for firing multiple rounds of ammunition in succession from a semiautomatic firearm."[30] Cottle transferred his patent to Slide Fire Solutions of Moran, Texas. The claims for that patent stated that Cottle's method of firing his bump stock utilized human muscle power to discharge each round while controlling the aim of the shooter. Part of the claims stated the invention functioned by "stabilizing an actuator in a stationary position relative to a second body part of the user *so that the firearm trigger will intermittently collide with the actuator* in response to linear reciprocating movement of the firing unit." [31] More patent lawyer legalese.

As with the Atkins bump stock, the shooter firing a semiautomatic fitted with a Cottle bump stock does not squeeze off shots with separate trigger pulls as he would when firing an unaltered semiautomatic. The trigger finger remains stationary. When the weapon is fired and recoils, forward pressure from the shooter's non-trigger-finger hand pulls the trigger forward so that the moving trigger will intermittently collide with the shooter's stationary trigger finger to fire succeeding rounds.

On June 7, 2010, John R. Spencer, chief of the ATF's firearms technology branch, wrote a letter responding to a request from Slide Fire Solutions asking that the ATF evaluate its bump stock, which the company claimed was intended to assist persons whose hands had limited mobility to bump fire an AR-15 type rifle.[32] By then the semiautomatic firearms ban had expired, so it was perfectly lawful to transfer and possess semiautomatic assault rifles again.

One would assume that as an ATF chief Spencer knew how a semiautomatic rifle functioned as well as the definition of a machine gun under the 1968 Act. He found that the stock "... had no automatically functioning mechanical parts or springs and performs no automatic mechanical function when installed. In order to use the installed device, the shooter must apply constant forward pressure with the non-shooting hand and constant rearward pressure with the shooting hand. Accordingly, we find that the bump-stock is a firearm part and is not regulated as a firearm under the Gun Control Act or the National Firearms Act."[33]

It was certainly true that the bump stock by itself could not fire any bullets. But if it was not a regulated firearm, then the Brady Act wouldn't apply, and no background check was necessary to purchase one. That should have given someone pause, but Spencer's letter did not discuss that or the fact that when a bump stock is attached to a semiautomatic rifle—its only purpose—the shooter's trigger finger remains stationary and the moving firearm trigger intermittently collides with it. Spencer's letter quoted in Chapter 7 did not discuss the distinction between an automatic and a semiautomatic firearm as defined by statute and articulated in the case law. The ATF must have known of that distinction. Nor did Spencer try to explain whether the method for firing multiple rounds of ammunition in succession from a semiautomatic firearm as described in the Cottle-Slide Fire Solutions patent,[34] was lawful under the 1968 law's definition of a machine gun.

Admittedly, one can argue that the operation of a semiautomatic fitted with a Slide Fire bump stock involves more than a single function of the trigger. However, the evil of a machine gun is that it discharges at a rate of hundreds of rounds a minute—and so can a semiautomatic fitted with a bump stock. Given the 1968 Act's language and intention, it is astounding that the ATF would authorize a part for a firearm that had no apparent purpose other than to convert a semiautomatic rifle into a machine gun-like firearm. Spencer's letter did not discuss the legality of a semiautomatic weapon fitted with a bump stock and an expanded magazine, the firing rate of such a weapon, whether he field tested a semiautomatic with a bump stock attached, nor whether a semiautomatic so fitted would be an unlawful machine gun as defined in the 1968 Act.

Other than Spencer's evaluation and letter, there were no other proceedings at the ATF nor was there any Congressional oversight of semiautomatic rifles fitted with a bump stock. Without the enactment of any new law following the Spencer letter, bump stocks were treated as lawful. Slide Fire Solutions proceeded to produce them, and gun dealers sold them into the civilian market.[35] Lawful firearms with machine gun-like capabilities had been reintroduced to the streets of America without one word from Congress.

On October 1, 2017, Paddock did not repeatedly pull the

trigger of his semiautomatics with his trigger finger at the Mandalay Bay Resort & Casino. His bump stocks cycled and continued to fire until the magazine was empty as long as he maintained forward pressure on the barrel with his non-trigger-finger hand. That is why the hail of bullets sounded *machine gun-like* to the concertgoers below the hotel. No human being has the physical ability to pull the trigger of semiautomatics at the rate Paddock discharged his bullets, estimated to be at a rate of more than 400 a minute.

News media after the Mandalay Massacre reported that some members of Congress had never even heard of a bump stock—nor had millions of Americans. Other members introduced legislation to ban it. Senator Dianne Feinstein (D-California), introduced a bill in the Senate to ban bump stocks.[36] Rep. Carlos Curbelo (R-Florida) and Seth Moulton (D-Massachusetts) introduced similar bipartisan measures in the House of Representatives. In response, NRA CEO Wayne LaPierre told CBS News's *Face the Nation* that the ATF should *do its job* and did not commit the NRA to supporting a legislated bump stock ban.[37] But by then in response to the Mandalay massacre bump stocks were flying off gun dealers' shelves. According to federal statutes on the books, the transfer or possession of a machine gun was a felony, but the transfer and possession of semiautomatics, extended loading devices, and bump stocks permitting the shooter to discharge bullets at a rate like that of a machine gun *were* lawful.

On December 26, 2018, the ATF issued a regulation (effective March 12, 2019) in response to a request from President Trump that banned the sale or possession of bump stocks like those used by the Mandalay Bay shooter. The regulation required that owners of bump stocks destroy them within 90 days by "crushing, melting, or shredding."[38] Gun Owners of America sued to enjoin enforcement of the regulation. Individual gun owners also challenged the regulation in Michigan claiming the regulation required the destruction of devices worth more than 100 million dollars. The Federal District Court for the Eastern District of Michigan refused to block the regulation and on appeal the U.S. Court of Appeals for the Sixth Circuit in Cincinnati rejected a request that the regulation be stayed during appeal. In a separate case the U.S. Court of Appeals for the District of Columbia did issue a stay pending appeal but its stay applied only to the plaintiffs in that case. When the plaintiffs in the latter case asked the U.S. Supreme Court to issue a broader stay[39] it refused to block the regulation during the appeal, but noted and did not disturb the D.C. Circuit partial ban. Litigation to overturn the federal bump stock ban is currently pending in a federal court in Austin, Texas.

On February 17, 2020, a bill that would have banned military styled weapons was defeated in the Virginia Senate. The bill would have banned the sale, purchase, manufacture and most transfers of military style weapons, large capacity magazines holding over 12 rounds, trigger activators, and bump stocks.[40] Later, in a chain of new laws Ralph Northam, the governor of the state of Virginia, signed into law new gun control measures over the weekend of April 11, 2020, including background check requirements and red flag laws that included the right to confiscate weapons from persons deemed dangerous to themselves or others.[41]

But should Congress or the ATF decide what constitutes a prohibited firearm? The ATF letter to Slide Fire Solutions approving the bump stock was not widely disseminated. Nor is there evidence the news media picked it up. Congress held no hearings to question the ATF's conclusions or to consider the legality of bump stocks. Nobody litigated the legality of bump stocks in the courts prior to 2019. The entire bump stock story demonstrates how our existing gun laws are ill-considered, fragmented measures that lack discipline and definition.

E. High velocity ammunition

We now confront an urgent need to control high-tech/high velocity ammunition that has no place in the civilian population. Efforts to do so have stalled. It was reported in *The New York Times* on August 10, 2019 that the victims of the terrorist shooting in El Paso, Texas suffered horrific injuries from the AK-47 that shooter used to fire high velocity ammunition. One surgeon interviewed for the article said, "She had two gaping holes the size of man's fist in her side and a third the size of a silver dollar where the bullet had burst from her body. Those bullets had also shredded her intestine." He said he reached into another wound and pulled out a bullet lodged in her shinbone. It had been flattened by its violent impact, "... into a disc the size of a quarter."[42] See also the discussion of similar surgeries performed, sometimes daily, in Detroit, Michigan in Chapter 14 below.

F. Brady Act background checks

The Brady Handgun Violence Prevention Act[43] (Brady Act), which requires background checks, is a valuable part of the federal statutory scheme. Although the Brady Act requires firearms buyers to pass background checks, Brady Act checks cannot weed out all killers.[44] It is now critical that Brady background checks be expanded to all points of sale, including gun shows, internet sales, and private sales, but current efforts to do so have stalled.

During 2018 the U.S. House of Representatives passed legislation with bi-partisan support to close loopholes in the Federal background check system that allowed, ". . . nearly a quarter of Americans who obtain firearms . . ." to obtain them without a background check. The Free Press reported that although "an overwhelming majority of Americans"[45] considered the Bill long overdue, Mitch McConnell, as of the close of February 2020, had refused to advance the House Bill to a vote in the Senate.

The *Detroit Free Press* reported in late 2019 that there had been a surge in background checks during 2019 as a result of a series of mass shootings, including the shootings in El Paso and Odessa, Texas and Dayton, Ohio, that left 38 people dead in August of 2019. The Free Press stated that the number of background checks for 2019 could break the one year record of 27.5 million according to FBI records, and that the single-day record was set two years earlier on "Black Friday" (the day after Thanksgiving) when a record 203,086 background check requests were made.[46]

G. Immunity from civil liability statutes

In response to civil suits against manufacturers and dealers, Congress enacted Public Law 109-92, euphemistically titled the Protection of Lawful Commerce in Arms Act, which went into effect October 26, 2005.[47] It protected firearms manufacturers and dealers from civil liability for damages for crimes committed by others with firearms that they had sold. The Act did not protect them from liability for defective products, breach of contract, criminal misconduct of their own, or negligent entrustment.[48] The Act created a special immunity for gun manufacturers and dealers that other manufacturers and dealers do not share.

In a case that may pierce the legal immunity of gun manufactures from civil liability, the United States Supreme Court ruled on November 12, 2019, that it would not hear an appeal by Remington Arms Company from a ruling by the Connecticut Supreme Court in *Soto vs. Bushmaster* that permitted a law suit by families of the Sandy Hook victims to proceed. The plaintiffs in the Soto case argued that the Bushmaster AR-15 used at Sandy Hook was advertised with phrases like, "Consider your man card reissued" and "The opposition will bow down" in violation of the Connecticut Unfair Trade Practices Act.[49]

H. Red Flag Laws

To deal with warning signs that gun violence is about to occur, some states have enacted red flag laws to prevent mentally disturbed individuals or domestic abusers from possessing firearms. Law enforcement or persons with a close relationship to the individual can request a court to issue a special restraining order to temporarily confiscate the individual's guns on the grounds of being a danger to themselves or others. Five states had red flag laws when the Stoneman Douglas attack occurred. Two more states, including Florida, have since adopted red flag laws. The Michigan legislature introduced House Bill No. 4706 (2017)[50] and Senate Bills 937 and 938 (2018)[51] but have not yet adopted them. According to some research red flag laws do more to prevent suicide than mass shootings.[52] Congress has failed to enact a red flag law.

Existing federal, state, and municipal laws have failed to control gun violence. If we rely on them the way forward looks bleak. Hundreds of proposed bills to bring gun violence under control have gone nowhere in Congress. Effective legislation dies in committee. If it reaches the floor, it is voted down. If enacted, it is "sunsetted," repealed, or ruled unconstitutional. It is common knowledge that each and every new proposal to regulate guns will be resisted by a determined, well-financed gun lobby that asserts the Founding Fathers guaranteed each citizen a right to bear arms when they placed the Second Amendment in the Bill of Rights.

But legislative inertia to the enactment of new statutes is not the whole story. As shown above, recent statutes and ordinances adopted at the federal, state, and local level to bring guns under more effective control have met fierce resistance in the courts. As shown in Chapters 3 and 4, when Washington, D.C., Chicago, and other cities, overwhelmed with violent homicide, enacted local ordinances to ban the possession of handguns within their city limits the Supreme Court announced in *Heller* and *McDonald* that "law-abiding citizens" had a constitutional right under the Second Amendment to possess a functional, unlocked handgun in their homes for self-defense that federal, state, and local government statutes or ordinances could not override. Those decisions are now the law of the land. Our legislative bodies are obligated to recognize a Second Amendment right to own and carry, but they have been left without a clear definition of what the right is or what laws and regulation they may adopt.

Following the Mandalay Bay massacre (described in Chapter 7), federal legislation to ban semiautomatics, high capacity magazines, and high velocity ammunition, stalled. The gun lobby and its adherents refuse to acknowledge that a whole lot more than the right of law-abiding citizens to defend themselves in their homes is involved. Nor do they concede that our Founding Fathers could not have foreseen the firepower of modern firearms or the population explosion that fills our society with social and economic tensions and strains law enforcement. Gun stores, army surplus stores, big boxes, e-mail outlets, and gun shows remain festooned with enough high-tech firepower to equip legions of law-abiding citizens. We do not live in the tranquility foreseen by the preamble to our Constitution.

There are over 20,000 gun control laws on the books at the state and local level in the United States although experts disagree on the exact figure.[53] Following the mass shooting at a theatre in Aurora, Colorado in 1912, law enforcement there was forced to concede that the shooter lawfully purchased the weapons he used. Incidents like Aurora, Columbine, Mandalay Bay, and Stoneman Douglas cry out for the enactment of new laws, and some responsible gun owners, gun manufacturers, and dealers have indicated a willingness to support such laws. But in today's political climate it is far from clear that any effective gun regulation can ever be enacted. Instead new laws are being proposed to expand the carriage of firearms.

Most states license handguns, but only a few state laws provide for background checks, regulate semiautomatics or extended loading devices, or contain red flag provisions. Following the Sandy Hook massacre in 2012, five states enacted laws expanding background checks to all points of sale (Florida, Oregon, Colorado, Connecticut, New York, Delaware, and Washington).[54] As of March 8, 2018, 18 states and Washington, D.C. had expanded their background check laws to all points of sale, but implementation varied from state to state.[55] Assault weapons bans have been enacted into law in California, Connecticut, Hawaii, Maryland, Massachusetts, New Jersey, and New York, and municipal assault weapons bans were enacted in the District of Columbia, Illinois, Indiana, and Massachusetts.[56] As of April 2019, Washington D.C. and nine U.S. states had high-capacity magazine restrictions or bans.[57] As of August 5, 2019, Red Flag laws (legislation that allows law enforcement to remove guns from individuals deemed to be a risk to themselves or others) had been enacted in 17 states, and proposed in 4 others.

Three people were killed, including two children, and 12 people were wounded in Gilroy, California on July 28, 2019, at the Gilroy Garlic Festival when a gunman armed with a semiautomatic rifle opened fire. California has some of the strictest gun laws in the nation. It was reported that the shooter purchased the semiautomatic in Nevada and carried it into California. Adam Skaggs, chief counsel of the Gilford's Law Center to Prevent Gun Violence, compared the transportation of guns across state lines to the air pollution problem. "Your state can be the strongest on regulating emissions, but if neighboring states have no pollution controls, the air pollution is going to come downwind."[58]

Because firearms are readily transportable, balkanized state regulation simply has not arrested the spread of firearms across state and city lines. This is true of New York City; it is also true of Chicago where suburban areas spill into Indiana and Wisconsin. Washington, D.C., abuts Maryland and Virginia. The San Diego-Tijuana and Detroit-Windsor regions straddle international borders. Known as the *Gunshine State* for its loose gun restrictions and widespread firearm ownership, Florida recently enacted gun control legislation to raise the minimum age to buy firearms and extended its waiting period to three days. The bill had bipartisan support and took only three weeks from introduction to law.[59] But no one state can establish effective gun regulation.

By elevating the right to bear arms to the status of a constitutional right belonging to private citizens, *Heller* encouraged legislation like these two bills by the Michigan Senate. In 2011, five senators introduced Bill No. 59 seeking to authorize the carriage of concealed handguns in virtually any public place including no-carry zones.[60] The bill passed both Houses of the Michigan legislature, but the Governor vetoed it. To date Michigan Law on open carry is not settled. In November 2017, little more than a month following the Mandalay Bay massacre, the Michigan Senate approved legislation to allow concealed handgun carry in sensitive places like schools, churches, and day care centers.[61] Teachers, parents, and the Michigan Education Association opposed the legislation.[62] The legislators apparently thought that the tragedy made the legislation timely because, "having responsibly armed gun owners in churches or schools could deter, stop, or minimize such attacks."[63]

These legislators wish to solve the gun problem through good guys with guns. But the notion that an even wider dispersal of firearms will solve the gun problem hasn't worked very well. Random gun shots on hunting lands out on the prairie are not the problem. Gun shots in sensitive places like schools, our city streets, and densely populated public areas are the problem. Military assault weapons with high velocity ammunition in the hands of civilians are the problem. Firearms in the hands of those unfit to have them are the problem. Good guys with guns will *not* solve these problems.

Congress is charged with the responsibility of protecting the rights of *all* U.S. citizens, not just those of gun owners. Those rights include the right to life and a right to live in domestic tranquility. Yet bills before Congress (in March 2018 following the shooting at Stoneman Douglas) include:[64]

- The STOP School Violence Act, which would authorize $50 million for safety improvements including training teachers and students how to prevent violence and develop anonymous reporting systems for threats of violence.

- A bill to provide schools with metal detectors and bulletproof doors.

- A bill to place bulletproof steel plates in the backpacks of school kids.

- A bill—submitted by Senator Lamar Alexander

(R-Tennessee)—to allow 100,000 schools to use federal funds to pay for school counselors, alarm systems, security cameras, and crisis intervention.

- A bill to improve reporting of gun purchases to the National Instant Criminal Background Check (NICS) system by offering incentives to states and federal agencies.

- One measure—deemed a health measure—would legalize silencers to protect against hearing impairment.

- The NRA pressed for concealed-carry reciprocity, which would allow people to carry concealed guns with them from places that permit them, such as Alaska, to any other part of the country.[65]

However, gun safety proposals to expand background checks to all points of sale, raise the minimum age to purchase a firearm, or to ban assault-style weapons like the AR-15, high capacity magazines, and bump stocks appear to be going nowhere on Capitol Hill. Legislation to furnish safety equipment to schools like metal detectors and security cameras, to arm the teachers or to hire guards ignores reality. While it's an attractive idea to have police forces or guards at schools to confront rampant gun violence, they're hardly a long-term solution to the nation's gun problem.

There are over 55 million students enrolled in more than 130,000 schools within the United States if you count all public, private, and parochial schools.[66] No one has explained how the cost of protecting our schools from gun violence through armed police or private guards can be met on a long-term basis when our schools are scrambling to find money to pay their teachers and staff. With only two guards for each school we'd be talking 260,000 guards. How would districts pay to train them? Who would supply their weapons? Who would supervise them? At $30,000 per year per guard it works out to 7.8 billion dollars per year *in salaries alone*, and two guards per school would hardly be adequate to protect 55 million students from semiautomatic rifles.

Recent reports indicated that Betsy DeVos, U.S. Secretary of Education, was considering a proposal to permit her department to divert funds from the Every Student Succeeds Act

(ESSA)—originally designated to help the nation's poorest schools with mental health counseling, dropout prevention, and re-entering students—to the purchase of guns and firearms training for school staffers.[67]

More to the point, arming teachers does nothing to deal with gun violence elsewhere. Proposals to place armed guards at schools—equal protection of the law considerations requires that all schools be included—can be seen for what they are: nothing but smoke screens to steer the national discussion away from principled laws that regulate highly dangerous firearms. It is axiomatic that the legal foundation for such laws must be predicated on the United States Constitution.

The next four chapters describe acts of brutal gun violence that existing laws like those described above have failed to control. It is a horrific toll of human lives destroyed, devastating injury and grief, and the perpetration of mass murder, school shootings, and terrorism unleashed.

6

Homicide, Suicide, and Domestic Violence

The blunt question these gatekeepers should ask clients or friends who seem troubled: "Is there a gun in your home?"

— *Catherine Barber, director of the Harvard Injury Control Research Center's Means Matter Campaign*

Too often we look away from the grim reality of gun violence. Blood-soaked incidents, one after the next, arising from gun violence have numbed our nation to the pain and anguish inflicted upon survivors and the victims' loved ones. Our leaders have stood wringing their hands as escalating gunfire explodes all around us and victims pile up. As painful and difficult as it is, the nation must examine the acts of gun violence that make America the leader of private gun ownership throughout the civilized world, and the place where thousands lost their lives or suffered severe injury from gunfire throughout our history. It is time to remember the victims and to contemplate the loss they have suffered.

A. Assassinations

1804: Vice President Aaron Burr mortally wounded former Secretary of the Treasury Alexander Hamilton in a duel at Weehawken, New York. Hamilton died the day after the duel.

1844: Joseph Smith, one of the founders of the Church of Latter-Day Saints (Mormons) and a presidential candidate, was shot by a mob while in jail under state protection.

1865: As the Civil War was winding down, President Abraham Lincoln, perhaps our greatest and certainly our most eloquent president, was relaxing in the President's box at Ford's Theatre in Washington, D.C. with his wife when a ball from a derringer fired by John Wilkes Booth, a Confederate sympathizer, pierced his head from behind. President Lincoln was about to undertake the reconstruction of our nation.

1881: President James Garfield died at a railroad station when struck by a bullet from a handgun fired by a disappointed office seeker.

1901: An anarchist firing a handgun fatally shot President William McKinley at the Pan American Exposition in Buffalo, New York.

1933: A bricklayer attempted to assassinate President-elect Franklin Delano Roosevelt with pistol shots. Five other people were hit, including Anton Cermak, the mayor of Chicago, who later died of his wound.

1950: Two Puerto Rican nationalists attempted to shoot their way into Blair House to assassinate President Harry S. Truman.

1963: A Ku Klux Klan member shot and killed Medgar Evers, a civil rights activist and NAACP leader.

1963: Lee Harvey Oswald fired a bullet from a mail-order rifle and splattered President John F. Kennedy's brain into the Presidential limousine in Dallas, Texas, while First Lady Jacqueline Kennedy sat horror-stricken by his side.

1965: Nation of Islam members shot Malcolm X while he was speaking at a rally in New York City.

1968: Dr. Martin Luther King was assassinated while standing on a motel balcony in Atlanta, Georgia during his campaign for civil rights. That bullet came from a rifle fired from an adjoining building.

1968: President Kennedy's brother, Senator Robert Kennedy, was exiting through a hotel kitchen in Los Angles, California after delivering a speech when Sirhan Sirhan fired a pistol, killing the Senator.

1975: Lynnette "Squeaky" Fromme fired at President Gerald Ford but missed.

1978: Dan White, a disgruntled ex-supervisor, slipped into the San Francisco City Hall and shot Mayor George Moscone and Supervisor Harvey Milk, one of the first openly gay elected officials. **1980:** John Lennon of the Beatles was shot by Mark David Chapman in New York City. Chapman fired five bullets at Lennon; four struck him in the back.

1981: John Hinckley shot and grievously wounded President Ronald Reagan at a hotel entrance in Washington, D.C.

2011: A gunman fired on the White House and hit the building at least seven times. That gunman was charged with attempting to assassinate President Barack Obama.

2011: Six were killed and U.S. Congresswoman Gabrielle "Gabby" Giffords along with 12 others shot during a constituent meeting held in a supermarket parking lot near Tucson, Arizona, by a man with a long history of mental illness.[1] According to reports, Jared Lee Loughner had exhibited strange behavior days before the shooting and purchased ammunition at a Walmart on the morning of the shooting.[2]

Eight out of 45 presidents have been killed, wounded, or shot at.

B. Homicide

Homicides committed with firearms occur daily across the United States. The 2011 *World Almanac* reported that more than 12,000 firearm homicides were committed in the United States during 2006.[3] A few examples that appear below inform us that homicide continues annually at crisis levels.

On November 13, 2011, the *Detroit Free Press* began publishing a special four-part series describing homicides committed in Detroit, Michigan.[4] It reported that Detroit led the nation in homicides per 1,000 residents, and 3,313 lives had been lost from January 2003 through November 2011. 83.4 percent died from gunshot wounds. The *Free Press* included a two-page map of the city, pinpointing the site of each killing.

The *Free Press* reported that 43 people were killed for every 100,000 residents in 2010, and the rate was trending at more than 50 for 2011. The victims were predominantly black men 18 to 44 years old. More Americans died in Detroit from homicide from 2003 to 2011 than had died in combat in Afghanistan up to that time. Detroit became known as the murder capital of America.

That carnage still goes on. From 2011 through 2016 the murder rate came down, but still averaged 335 murders per year. In a 24-hour period in Detroit, May 15–16, 2013, 13 people were shot, one fatally. Detroit authorities have organized a Counter Terrorist Threat Assessment Team (including police, fire, and hospital personnel) that regularly trains to meet threats of mass shootings in the city. In response to the shooting at Parkland, Florida the FBI reorganized its Detroit Joint Terrorism Task Force to consolidate efforts to collect reports of mass shooting threats previously spread over several squads.[5]

Recently Chicago, Illinois, supplanted Detroit as the murder capital of America. Chicago reported 762 homicides and 4,368 shooting victims from January 1 through December 31, 2016.[6] 13 people died of gunshot wounds over the 2016 Labor Day weekend, and at least 52 others received gunshot wounds. Three children were shot and killed in Chicago during a four-day period in February of 2017.[7] Chicago police attributed the increase to the easy availability of guns and gang violence.[8] During a 60-hour period over the weekend of August 4–5, 2018, at least 72 people were shot in Chicago—12 fatally. By the end of July, Chicago had recorded 300 gunshot murders during 2018, more than any other U.S. city.[9] And now Baltimore, Maryland, may contend for the murder capital title.[10]

But homicide continues apace across our nation. The FBI annual *Crime in the United States, 2015*[11] reported that there had been 15,696 murders committed that year in America. Firearms accounted for 71.5 percent of the murders. It's not surprising that the widespread disbursal of firearms in our communities, homicide, and the parade of mass shootings have created enormous problems for state and municipal police. In July of 2016, following protests over police shootings in Minnesota and Louisiana, Micah Xavier Johnson, who was reportedly planning even larger attacks, shot five police officers dead in Dallas, Texas.[12] In all 18 police officers were killed by gun violence within the United States during the period from January 1, 2016, to July 28, 2016.[13]

On June 10, 2016, *The New York Times* published an article describing five gangland-style shootings that occurred in 2015, killing and wounding innocent bystanders.[14]

– February 6, Tulsa, Oklahoma. Barbers were cutting hair and kibitzing with their customers when a gang member armed with an AK-47 tried to take out a rival getting a haircut. Instead, he shot dead one of the barbers and wounded three people. The target shot the gunman's accomplice and wounded him.

- May 10, Newark, New Jersey. Sherkimea Zigler, fifteen, who played on his school's football and basketball teams and had made the honor roll, was killed in the crossfire between two rival gangs at an outdoor motorcycle exhibition. Sherkimea had just called his mother to wish her a happy Mother's Day.

- June 11, Bridgeport, Connecticut. Residents were seated chatting and listening to music in a parking lot when gang members armed with semiautomatic handguns appeared and opened fire. One resident died when at least 19 bullets struck him. Eight others were wounded. The irony was that the assailants opened fire in the wrong parking lot; their target was in the next lot.

- June 21, Lexington, Kentucky. Several gunmen began shooting from both sides of a basketball court. A food truck owner was killed, and four others were wounded.

- August 1, Orlando, Florida. An argument broke out in a parking lot adjoining an apartment building. Ten-year-old Victor Hernandez lost an eye when hit by a bullet coming through his apartment window from a nine-millimeter handgun. Three others were wounded.

By 2017, we had become a nation at war with ourselves. On October 9, 2017, *The New York Times* published a startling graphic listing daily shooting deaths (1,102), with the number of victims per incident in 19 major U.S. cities during 2017 up to October 1.[15] The list, compiled from data furnished by the Gun Violence Archive, showed the number of days it took in each major city to equal the 58 killed by the Mandalay Bay shooter. Chicago took the shortest number of days at 28, while Baton Rouge took the longest at 198 days. Statistics like these make you wonder if anybody is listening or paying attention to the horrific consequences of our refusal to sensibly regulate firearms.

On December 6, 2019, *The New York Times* published an article on the increase in gang related shootings in the city of New York. The article noted that although crime overall had been reduced in the city, ". . . gun violence has flared up in some pockets of the metropolis, focusing attention on youth gangs with access to firearms, a combination that often turns deadly."[16]

On New Year's Day in 2020, shootings erupted across the nation. In St. Louis, Missouri, a teenage boy was shot in the leg; minutes later four more persons were shot—three fatally, and the police were investigating 10 shootings. In Cleveland, Ohio, a man shooting his weapon to celebrate the New Year accidentally killed his girlfriend. In Orlando, Florida, two men were killed in a shooting at a nightclub. In Baltimore the police were investigating two killings. In Houston, Texas, a 61-year old woman was killed by a stray bullet. In Lubbock, Texas, two people were killed in a shooting outside a nightclub. In Philadelphia two people were killed on New Year's Eve. A man and a woman were shot and wounded at a bar in South Bend, Indiana. A 14-year-old boy was shot and killed in Des Moines, Iowa.[17]

C. Suicide and Domestic Violence

More people commit suicide with a gun than are killed by other people with a gun.[18]

Suicide has reached epidemic proportions as the tenth leading cause of death in the United States. 38,364 people killed themselves in 2010. In more than half of these cases a firearm was used.[19] In 2017, suicide by gun deaths totaled 23,854.[20]

During 2015, 1,686 women died as a result of domestic homicide. Firearms were the weapon most commonly used.[21] Federal legislation to deal with this problem has been stalemated. On April 4, 2019, The House of Representatives passed HR 1585, the Violence Against Women Reauthorization Act of 2019. That Act reauthorized the Violence Against Women Act of 1984 (42 U.S.C. sections 13701 through 14040), expanded the ability of law enforcement personnel to restrict gun purchases by domestic abusers, and expanded the provisions of the 1994 Act to close the so-called boyfriend loophole. Because of provisions that would strip domestic abusers of their guns, the NRA opposed HR 1585 in the House of Representatives and threatened to "score" those who voted for it. It was sent to the Senate but to date has not passed in that body.[22]

While the causes of suicide and domestic abuse are multiple and beyond the scope of this book, the fact that guns are lethal and easily accessible accounts for guns being the weapon of choice for suicide victims and domestic abusers. Red Flag laws won't solve these two problems, but they would help. They could give other occupants of homes and co-workers of potential suicide victims or abusers broader power to alert law enforcement or mental health providers that a potential suicide victim or abuser has access to firearms. They could also provide cover for those reporting acts that may lead to the use of firearms for suicide or domestic violence.

CHAPTER 7

The Mandalay Bay Massacre

It's a hell of a thing, killing a man. You take away everything he's got and everything he's ever gonna have.

—Clint Eastwood, UNFORGIVEN

It was the best of times; it was the worst of times.[1] Incidents like the Mandalay Bay massacre exemplify the carnage that unregulated firearms inflict upon the civilian population and reveal that the failure of our elected leaders to enact responsible common sense firearm laws is no longer acceptable.

On Sunday, October 1, 2017, high-stakes gambler Stephen Paddock was alone in his suite on the 32nd floor of the Mandalay Bay Resort and Casino in Las Vegas amid an arsenal of 23 firearms and hundreds of rounds of ammunition he had hauled into his room inside suitcases. He was not on a hunting trip, and he did not assemble his weapons for defense of hearth or home. Paddock's arsenal included 12 semiautomatic rifles with high capacity magazines and bump stocks* he could attach to his semiautomatics.

Bump stocks were certainly not well-regulated—indeed, not regulated at all. Relatively new to the civilian market, their existence and purpose weren't widely known, although thousands had been sold. But with those bump stocks attached to his semiautomatics, Paddock knew he could fire machine gun-like bursts

---

*An attachment that makes a semiautomatic firearm, like an AR-15 rifle, shoot nearly as fast as fully automatic machine guns. It replaces the standard rifle stock with a piece of plastic or metal molded to the lower end of the gun. It uses the recoil to fire shots more rapidly than possible with single trigger pulls. *See* more extensive discussion in Chapter 5, "The bump stock story" above.

and inflict massive damage. A photograph in later press reports showed a glove on his left hand. Gloves are hardly necessary in Las Vegas, but Paddock also knew machine gun-like bursts heat up the barrel of a semiautomatic. Paddock had a well-thought-out plan. Everything was set to go. Whatever logic there might be in Justice Scalia's carefully crafted opinion in *Heller,*[2] it was light-years away from Paddock's purposes.

The windows of Paddock's suite had a clear view of the Route 91 Harvest Festival of 22,000 happy country music lovers in the cool desert air and electric atmosphere of the Vegas Strip. They were mostly young Americans enjoying a magnificent evening with their favorite performers. The Mandalay Bay's windows formed a glimmering, golden backdrop to the festival, perhaps reminiscent of the notion that America is a shining city on a hill. Paddock was invisible to any pain in the ass festival patrons gawking up at the Mandalay Bay or shooting cellphone photographs. He was in his hunting blind; the music fans were sitting ducks.

According to reports, at about ten o'clock that Sunday evening, with country music filling the air and entrancing the crowd below, Paddock picked up a hammer, smashed out two of the windows, and proceeded to spray bullets from upgraded semiautomatic rifles into the crowd. The staccato *dut-dut-dut* of Paddock's weapons blended into the music of Jason Aldean's band.

Festival goers first thought it was firecrackers and part of the show. A police officer in the area didn't—it sounded like machine gun fire to him, as it did to others later. The *dut-dut-dut* heard on television from video taken that night sounded like the machine gun fire heard in gangster and war movies.

Hey, wait a minute; that couldn't be. Machine guns are illegal under federal statutes, aren't they? Isn't it a felony to transfer or possess machine guns?

The Harvest Festival was under attack by what sounded like military assault weapons. Bullets whizzed all around the open-air theater. Screaming fans fell to the ground, their wounds gushing blood. They didn't know where the bullets were coming from or how many shooters there were. No time to think, let alone stand your ground. Their beloved festival was a war zone.

Panicked concertgoers stampeded in all directions, unsure where to run or find cover. Some took a bullet when they stopped to aid others lying on the ground, drenched in blood. Some with battlefield or EMT experience applied pressure to wounds and improvised tourniquets. Some tried to shield loved ones and even strangers with their own bodies. The stampede fleeing the scene blocked first responders and emergency workers trying to locate the source of the fusillade and the shooter or shooters.

The attack continued for over ten minutes. There were reports of wounded people in neighboring hotel lobbies where they had fled, leading the first responders to believe they were under an orchestrated attack by terrorists at several Las Vegas hotels—another 9/11. The shooting stopped by 10:17 when police officers arrived outside the 32nd floor suite. When they blew the locked door away at 11:20, they found Paddock dead on the floor from a self-inflicted bullet through his head.

Fifty-eight people died at the scene or on the way to trauma centers because medical help couldn't get to them fast enough. It was later reported that 851 people were wounded in the shooting, 422 of them by gunfire. Some several times.[3] Gunshot wounds from semiautomatic weapons and high velocity ammunition are far deadlier than those from ordinary handguns. Bullets from an M16 or AR-15 depart the muzzle at a velocity of more than 3,000 feet per second. Limbs are sheared off, bones are shattered, and organs are destroyed.[4] Bullets from common handguns have half to a third of that speed.

Most hurricanes and wildfires cause fewer casualties than the Mandalay Bay massacre did. The EMTs and first responders were overwhelmed. There weren't enough ambulances or stretchers to transport all the victims. Bodies were carried and loaded onto truck beds and back seats of cars and carted off to emergency rooms. Later, a makeshift memorial of flowers and photographs sprang up near the scene of the massacre, at the iconic Welcome to Las Vegas sign. White crosses commemorated the dead.

It happened in the United States of America, the shining city on a hill, sweet land of liberty, the land of the free and home of the brave, where massacres don't invade country music festivals. But it did happen. It all happened in a nation whose Declaration of Independence declared that all men are endowed with certain unalienable rights including the right to life, liberty, and the pursuit of happiness, and "that to secure these rights, Governments are instituted among men." After the worst mass shooting in America's history, you would assume that Congress, emulating the first re-sponders at Mandalay Bay, would finally spring into action, right?

But it also happened after the U.S. Supreme Court inter-preted the Second Amendment to create a *private* right to bear firearms, however ill-defined. It happened when Brady Act back-ground checks could not weed out all mass killers, when Congress had said semiautomatic rifles and extended-loading devices were lawful firearms, and when the ATF determined that Slide Fire So-lutions's bump stock was not subject to regulation because it was not a firearm.

Investigators later discovered that from 1982 through the fall of 2017, Paddock acquired more than 80 firearms and over 100 related items such as bump stocks, scopes, and ammunition. Las Vegas Metropolitan Police Department photographs published by the *Telegraph* showed 23 guns and attachments strewn around his suite.[5] It was reported later that one of the dealers who sold Paddock his weapons said that Paddock had passed all his Brady tests. Gun rights supporters may claim that semiautomatics with high capacity magazines and bump stocks are not machine guns and therefore perfectly legal. But our legislators and leaders failed all who were murdered or maimed at the music festival and their loved ones. They failed all of us.

Recall that, as explained in Chapter 5 above, in 1994 Con-gress enacted an amendment to the 1968 Act that, among other things, provided, "It shall be unlawful for a person to manufac-ture, transfer, or possess a semiautomatic assault weapon."[6] It also made it unlawful for a person "to transfer or possess a large capac-ity feeding device."[7] Of course the gun lobby saw to it that there were exceptions, including weapons lawfully possessed before the Act took effect,[8] together with hundreds of firearms identified and exempted in Appendix A[9] to the Act. The 1994 Act also excepted any "semiautomatic rifle *that cannot accept* a detachable magazine that holds more than five rounds of ammunition."[10] This was a backward way of saying that transfer and possession of semiauto-matics that could accept such a clip were felonies under the 1994 Act. Inexplicably, a sunset provision in the 1994 Act provided that the semiautomatic weapons ban would expire ten years following September 13, 1994, the date of its enactment, unless renewed by Congress.[11]

The gun lobby sure did its job. Congress did not renew, so

the semiautomatic assault rifle ban quietly expired in 2004. Had the 1994 ban stayed in effect, it would have been a felony and far more difficult for Paddock to have semiautomatic rifles unless he possessed them before the 1994 Act took effect. Why would legislators enact a semiautomatic firearms felony *on the grounds that semiautomatics are highly dangerous weapons*, sunset it, and never look back?

As we shall see, anyone who believed that the Mandalay Bay shooting taught us our lesson was sadly mistaken. Our history with guns created a culture and political climate in which sane regulation was abandoned to satisfy a near pathologic craving for guns with increased firepower. Part of the cost of that craving emerged on October 4, 2019, when MGM Resorts International, the owner of the Mandalay Bay hotel, reportedly agreed to pay up to $800 million to settle lawsuits filed by victims of that mass shooting.[12] As the next three chapters show, long before the settlement of those Mandalay Bay claims ever happened, gun regulation, gun violence, and mass murder in America had become a gut-wrenching farce of politics, money, and blood all the way down.

CHAPTER 8

A Litany of Mass Murder

You know, you know, you can't talk to a man
With a shotgun in his hand.

— *Carole King, SMACKWATER JACK*

Mandalay Bay is hardly an outlier. Driven by social rejection or emotional problems a mass murderer will fire multiple rounds upon crowds of innocent people to strike back at society or to make a personal or political statement. Most mass murders defy rational explanation.

The modern era of mass shootings and legislative inaction commenced in 1966 when Charles Whitman, a student at the University of Texas in Austin, went up to the campus clock tower's observation deck with a rifle and fired upon those below at random for an hour and a half until he was killed by police. In all 16 people were killed and more than 30 wounded by the Texas Tower Sniper.

In the 21st century the pace of mass shootings quickened. For three weeks in October 2002, two snipers—41-year-old John Allen Muhammad and his 17-year-old accomplice, Lee Boyd Malvo—terrorized commuters in Maryland, Virginia, and Washington, D.C. They shot and killed ten people and critically wounded three more in the Beltway sniper attacks.[1]

Over five months in 2003 and 2004, Charles McCoy, Jr. fired at drivers on I-270 near Columbus, Ohio, killing one. Hardly a mass killing, but it had all the earmarks of becoming one. A diagnosed paranoid schizophrenic, he was sentenced to 27 years in prison in a plea bargain.[2]

On April 16, 2007, Seung-Hui Cho, a student with a history of mental illness, shot 32 students and faculty members to death and wounded 17 others at Virginia Polytechnic Institute in Blacksburg, Virginia, before taking his own life.[3]

While these mass shootings made big headlines, they were only the tip of the iceberg. Given readily available firearms, only a cretin would have thought mass murder would never happen again.

And it did at a midnight showing of *The Dark Knight Rises* at a theatre in Aurora, Colorado, on July 20, 2012. James Holmes, a 24-year-old former honors doctoral student who later told police he was the Joker, entered the theatre wearing tactical body armor, brandishing a Smith & Wesson AR-15 assault rifle, a shotgun, and two Glock pistols, and armed with over 6,000 rounds of ammunition he had purchased on the Internet. He fired into the audience, killing 12 and wounding 58.[4] If a good guy with a gun had tried to stop him per the standard NRA recommendation, he would have been dead meat.[5]

A former naval reservist, Aaron Alexis, from Fort Worth, Texas, with a history of infractions, shot his way into the naval office building at the Washington Navy Yard in Washington, D.C, on September 16, 2013, killing 12 people. Police officers shot and killed him.[6]

On June 12, 2016, 49 people were killed at the Pulse, a gay night club in Orlando, Florida. The gunman, Omar Mateen, who claimed allegiance to the Islamic State, was killed in a gun battle with police who stormed the club. Bodies lay atop one another. The *New York Times* described this massacre as the worst mass shooting in United States history. Mateen had come armed with an assault rifle and a pistol.

Following the Orlando massacre Congressional Democrats staged a sit-in on the floor of the House of Representatives to force a discussion on the lack of gun reform. Instead the United States Senate blocked four measures to curb gun sales, including proposals to bar the sale of guns to terrorism suspects and to those on the no-fly list, and to tighten background checks for buyers at gun shows or over the Internet. In February of 2017 Congress struck down an administrative rule that President Obama had adopted to prevent persons with severe mental problems from buying guns.[7] Congress had to know that without effective regulation the carnage was going to spread from sea to shining sea. And it sure did.

June 14, 2017: James Thomas Hodgkinson, allegedly distraught over the election of Donald Trump as president and events following his inauguration, fired on a baseball team of Republican congressmen practicing in Alexandria, Virginia, wounding five.[8] Two Capitol police officers killed the assailant who was armed with an assault rifle and a pistol. Some claimed the incident proved that what stops a bad guy with a gun is a good guy with a gun. None suggested that what might stop a bad guy with a gun is a good guy with a law.

On November 5, 2017, the parishioners of the First Baptist Church in Sutherland Springs, Texas, had assembled for the Sunday service. With a population of about 16,000, Sutherland Springs is a peaceful, close-knit small town where church activities play a central role in community and family life. First Baptist is a congregation of families, married couples, neighbors, and friends; many have lived there for most of their lives. Among them was the pastor's daughter, 14-year-old Annabelle Pomeroy. The Holcombe family was there, including Bryan, a guest preacher, his wife Karla, their son Marc Daniel, their daughter Crystal, who was expecting her first child, her husband John, and four grandchildren.

During the service Devin Patrick Kelley, a 26-year-old sometime congregant at First Baptist and former member of the United States Air Force, drove up to the church. Kelley got out of his vehicle carrying a Ruger AR-15-type semiautomatic rifle and several clips to reload. He approached the front entrance and began firing bullets through the door and into the walls of the church. Dressed in all-black tactical gear and wearing a mask, he shot parishioners, loading his rifle with new clips as he walked down the center aisle. He shot children in the head at point blank range, including the pastor's daughter Annabelle. He shot and killed eight members of the Holcombe family, including Crystal's fetus. The shooting continued for almost seven minutes. In all he shot and killed 26 parishioners and wounded 20 others. *The New York Times* reported that officers described the scene as one of "unfathomable carnage." and "wherever you walked there was death."[9]

Kelley left the church and fled when a neighbor began to shoot at him. Wounded, Kelley ran to his vehicle and sped out of town. Kelley was found at a crash site with three gunshot wounds including a bullet to his head, self-inflicted.

Following the massacre the church was closed. The pews

were removed, and folding chairs took their place. Red roses were placed on the chairs with names of the victims. White crosses were placed outside the church, and the following Sunday services were held in a tent pitched outside the church building. Politicians made their usual remarks expressing horror, grief, and condolences that so many had been killed and wounded. Few of them mentioned that an unregulated semiautomatic had not only destroyed the lives of half of First Baptist's parishioners, but it had rendered the church building they struggled to build and support uninhabitable.

President Trump, on a trip to Asia, said the shooting at Sutherland Springs was not related to the regulation of gun ownership, and that "mental health is your problem here." So much for the ability of background checks to provide mental health screening. Some gun rights promoters commented that the massacre at Sutherland Springs proved the value of having a good guy with a gun present.

The church regularly videotaped its services. The massacre was recorded on tape leaving no doubt that it was the worst mass murder in Southern Texas history. Coming 36 days after Mandalay Bay, the massacre at Sutherland Springs rattled the nation again. A litany of incidents too numerous to list confirmed that even though machine guns were banned, semiautomatic rifles and handguns can discharge multiple rounds *in seconds*. These incidents also proved that military assault-style weapons and ammunition are easily available to those unfit to have or carry them into public places. Americans were no longer safe at country music festivals held in Fun City, and they were no longer safe in the pews of a church in Southern Texas.

Kelley was able to acquire his weapons after passing Brady Act background checks he should have failed. It was reported the day after the massacre that while in the Air Force Kelley had been convicted of domestic abuse of his wife and daughter and court-martialed. The Air Force admitted that it failed to notify the FBI. Had the conviction and court-martial been reported, Kelley would never have been cleared to purchase the Ruger AR-15 he used to gun down the parishioners.

On June 28, 2018, Jarrod Ramos, armed with a shotgun and smoke grenades, attacked the Capital Gazette newsroom in Annapolis, Maryland, shot five journalists to death and wounded two others.[10] Ramos reportedly had had a legal dispute with the newspaper over a 2011 column about his harassment of a former high school classmate.

A few months later another shooting stunned the nation. One day after the election, on November 7, 2018, college students were line dancing and shooting pool during College Country Night at the Borderline Bar & Grill in Thousand Oaks, California. Until a man clad in black, reportedly a former Marine who served in Afghanistan and suffered from post-traumatic stress syndrome, entered the bar armed with smoke grenades and an automatic pistol equipped with a high capacity magazine. He opened fire into the crowd of over 100 people, killing 12 and wounding upwards of 22 others. One fatality, Telemachus Orfanos, had attended the country music Route 91 Harvest Festival in Las Vegas the year before and survived that massacre. Following the Borderline Bar massacre, his mother, Susan Schmidt-Orfanos, said to an interviewer, "He didn't come home last night, and the two words I want you to write are: gun control—right now—so that no one else goes through this. Can you do that? Can you do that for me? Gun control."[11]

In August of 2019, there were reports of threatened mass shootings across three states. The alleged perpetrator in Connecticut was arrested on charges of possession of large capacity magazines and for allegedly posting threats to commit mass murder. The arrestee in Florida allegedly texted threats to commit mass murder, including one that read, "But a good 100 kills would be nice." In Ohio the arrestee was charged with telecommunications harassment involving alleged threats against a Jewish Community Center and possession of semiautomatic weapons.[12]

On August 3, 2019, hours after the mass shooting at an El Paso, Texas, Walmart, a man wearing body armor walked into a bar in Dayton, Ohio, carrying a semiautomatic rifle and shot 9 people dead, including his sister, and wounded a dozen others.[13] On Saturday, August 31, 2019, part of the Labor Day weekend, a gunman armed with an AR-15 style semiautomatic weapon and firing from his vehicle and later a stolen mail van, shot seven people to death and wounded 25 others, including three law enforcement officers, in a shooting spree along a 15 mile stretch of highways and shopping malls between Midland and Odessa, Texas. The dead ranged in age from 15 to 57. One of the victims, a 17-month old girl, was reported to be recovering from surgery to repair injuries to her face, teeth, and chest inflicted by shrapnel. It was reported that the gunman had been recently fired from his job. He was killed in a shootout with police officers. No evidence of a domestic or foreign terrorist plot appeared in the initial reports.[14]

There were two shootings at military bases in late 2019. On Wednesday, December 4, 2019, a sailor in Hawaii shot and killed two shipyard workers and wounded another at the Pearl Harbor Naval Shipyard, and on Friday, December 6, 2019, a Saudi Trainee shot three people dead at a Naval Air Station in Pensacola, Florida. These shootings followed two shootings at a military base in Fort Hood in Texas (one in 2009 where 12 military personnel and 1 civilian were killed and another in 2014 when 3 soldiers were killed and 12 others were wounded).[15]

On Sunday, December 29, 2019, a gunman armed with a shotgun opened fire at the West Freeway Church of Christ in White Settlement, Texas, killing one person before armed parishioners fired back and killed the gunman. Had the parishioners not acted it would have been a mass shooting and the death total would have been much higher.[16]

On Sunday, February 16, 2020, three citizens and one police officer were killed in a mass shooting in Springfield, Missouri. Another police officer was wounded. The attacker was found dead from self-inflicted gunshot wounds.[17]

The *Detroit Free Press* reported a data base had been compiled by the Associated Press, USA Today, and Northeastern University, that disclosed more mass killings in 2019 than any year since the 1970's. It reported that there were 41 mass killings, defined as when four or more people are killed, during 2019. [18]

In what police described as an anti-Semitic hate crime and an act of domestic terrorism, four people including a police officer and the two assailants were killed at a kosher market operated by a Hasidic Jewish family in Jersey City, New Jersey, on Tuesday, December 10, 2019.[19]

April Zeoli, associate professor of criminal justice at Michigan State University and lead author of research on the extent to which mass shootings are committed by domestic violence perpetrators recently stated, "We found that 38% of known mass shooters had a history of domestic violence, either known to the justice system or mentioned in the media . . . "[20]

As you ponder these massacres and the carnage described on these pages, consider that public officials and ordinary citizens continue to promote an unfettered Second Amendment right to own and carry semiautomatic assault weapons, bump stocks, and extended loading devices. Some assert—*Guns don't kill people, people kill people.*

You reach the point where you just can't stand looking at all the news reports or even hearing about it anymore. You want to scream. You want to throw up your hands or turn away. But *ALL* of us have a responsibility to bear witness, to speak up, to do something—or else how and when will it stop? We cannot let our leaders off the hook and permit them to sweep gun violence under the rug. They ought to lead. They ought to mold public opinion into accepting rational controls. *It's their job.* Even if gun violence and its toll described in the previous chapters are not enough, those in the next chapter on school shootings make it indelibly clear that we need new gun laws.

CHAPTER 9

Parkland and Other School Shootings

Violence isn't always evil. What's evil is the infatuation with violence.

—Jim Morrison

School shootings are a special breed of mass shootings. They are horrifying because the victims are trusting grade school and high school students innocently sitting in their classrooms being taught the American dream. The introduction of semiautomatic weapons, extended loading devices, and high tech ammunition and explosives into that environment is totally beyond the pale.

Consider that in 1999, two seriously disturbed students, Eric Harris, 18, and Dylan Klebold, 17, executed a planned attack at Columbine High School in Colorado, killing 12 students and adults and wounding 21 others. They also planted bombs, most of which failed to explode. Their arsenal included a Hi-point 995 Carbine, a Savage 67HK pump action shotgun, a Stevens 311D double-barreled sawed-off shotgun, and a 995 Carbine semiautomatic handgun. They fired a total of 176 rounds, including the two shots they used to kill themselves.[1] The perpetrators were both underage and had felony records, yet they were still able to acquire their arsenal, some of which a friend of theirs purchased at a gun show in December 1998. No new national gun laws resulted.

Then 12 years later, in less than five minutes on December 14, 2012, Adam Lanza shot and killed 20 schoolchildren between the ages of six and seven years old along with six faculty members at the Sandy Hook Elementary School in Newtown, Connecticut. His weapon was a semiautomatic Bushmaster XM-15 assault rifle.[2] Lanza had amassed a cache of guns, swords, knives, and ammunition at his home in Newtown. Again, no new gun laws.

On January 23, 2018, two 15-year-old students were shot and killed, and 17 more people were wounded by gunfire at a high school in Benton, Kentucky. In an article discussing the Benton incident, *The New York Times* reported that researchers had logged school shooting incidents since 2013 at the rate of about one per week,[3] and that 11 shootings involving schools had occurred in the first 23 days of 2018. Even then, no new laws. What would it take?

Then, on Valentine's Day 2018, which was also Ash Wednesday, before the 2017 mass shootings at Mandalay Bay and Sutherland Springs had settled into the national memory, another school shooting generated screaming national headlines. This time it happened at the Marjory Stoneman Douglas High School in Parkland, Florida, a suburb of Fort Lauderdale with a population of about 30,000. The alleged gunman, Nikolas Cruz, was a former student who had been expelled as a disciplinary problem.

Wearing a gas mask, carrying smoke grenades, and brandishing an AR-15 semiautomatic rifle, Cruz set off the fire alarms around 2:40 p.m., just before the end of the school day, to lure those in attendance out into the open. As the students and teachers exited in response to the fire alarm, Cruz opened fire. Then he walked through the school firing at anyone he encountered. Students sought refuge in their classrooms, hiding under desks or in closets.

Police officers raced to the scene not knowing how many shooters there were and asked students to leave the building with their hands over their heads to show they had no weapons. Terrified teachers told students to leave in lines and to place their hands on the shoulder of the student ahead of them as they were led away. School cameras recorded screaming and crying students running from their school. The slaughter in some classrooms was video recorded by students on their cell phones, revealing scenes of absolute devastation.

Seventeen students and teachers were shot dead, 14 others wounded and taken to nearby hospitals. One teacher was killed as he shielded students from harm. 15-year-old Anthony Borges slammed and blocked a door to keep the shooter away from a classroom where his classmates were huddled in fear. Borges was shot five times in his legs and torso. He was taken to a hospital and though grievously wounded survived.[4] Madness!

Cruz abandoned his weapons in a stairwell and melted into the hordes of students fleeing from the school. Identified by a red shirt he was wearing, he was arrested in Coral Springs an hour later. When horrified parents came to the school to find their children, not knowing if they were dead or alive, some were told not to use cell phones because a ringing phone might identify the place their child was hiding.

Currently, many recommend the use of armed officers or private police at our schools.[5] Armed officers on duty at Stoneman Douglas at the time of the shooting were severely criticized for not confronting the shooter, but it was later pointed out that they would have had to confront a long-range semiautomatic with short-range side arms.

Once again, the mass shooting at Stoneman Douglas prompted a rush to purchase firearms across the nation. Thousands attended a gun and knife show in Novi, Michigan, on February 24, 2018, ten days after Stoneman Douglas. One vendor there reportedly sold everything from handguns to lever action rifles to semiautomatic rifles. A patron was reported to have said, "People think right or wrong: *Oh, they're going to ban this or legislate this.* And then there is a reaction. It's a natural instinct."[6]

It should have been a federal felony for Kelley to acquire and carry a Ruger AR-15 into the First Baptist Church and for Cruz to acquire and carry one into the Stoneman Douglas High School. Even if they acted as a result of mental instability, it should have been a federal felony for gun dealers to place AR-15 semiautomatics and the ammunition for them into Kelley's and Cruz's hands. As shown above, their semiautomatics had been banned in 1994. Congress allowed the ban to expire and refused to renew it. The awkward truth behind those massacres is that politicians kowtow to the gun lobby. There is no way to sugar coat it. Our politicians are bought and paid for.

Following the massacre at Parkland, Florida, the traumatized students from Stoneman Douglas and their parents let it be known that this time it was going to be different. While struggling with their enormous loss, they attended a meeting with

President Trump, other political leaders, and the media a few days following the massacre, where they grippingly expressed the terror they had experienced and their grief, and boldly offered ideas on how to prevent such massacres. The passion of the students and their parents who attended that meeting exploded in bold relief when one father, trying to hold back his tears, told the President that the only place left for him to visit his daughter was the cemetery. He told the President of the United States point blank that he was pissed.

Later President Trump suggested to those at the meeting that the answer was to arm the teachers. Many of the students and their parents did not think that was a good idea. Instead they drove to Florida's capital in Tallahassee to express their outrage at the massacre and to demand new laws to protect Florida schools and to control dangerous firearms. The Stoneman Douglas teenagers, who spoke with President Trump and later on television from Tallahassee, were highly energized, intelligent, and well-spoken high school students demanding common sense gun controls and justice. They spoke like the young adults they were. When they arrived in Tallahassee, they discovered that many of the legislators they wanted to confront were no-shows. They were staying well away from the grief-stricken but outraged students. Rebuffed, the teens took to television to voice their demands and then turned their sights on Washington, D.C.

Within days of the massacre, the Stoneman Douglas students met with some success. On March 9, 2018, Governor Rick Scott signed a bill quickly adopted by the Florida legislature to, among other things, raise the minimum age for purchasing a gun to 21, extend the waiting period for purchasing a gun to three days, impose restrictions on bump stocks, and to provide police protection and mental health services for schools. It was not all they were asking for and hardly enough. Still, the rage of the Stoneman Douglas teens proved to be a game changer. The NRA, true to form, immediately filed a lawsuit to have parts of the new Florida statutes declared unconstitutional.

On March 14, 2018, students from all over the nation walked out of their classrooms as part of the National School Walkout protest in support of the Stoneman Douglas students. Articles that appeared in *The New York Times* on March 14, 2018,[7] including a guest editorial by three New Jersey high school teens, confirm that the movement started by the Stoneman Douglas teens was going national. Some Stoneman Douglas students appeared on CBS News, *60 Minutes* on March 18, 2018, and later on MSNBC. A movement was forming. You could sense it.

A Never Again Movement and a March for Our Lives erupted. Over a million students assembled from all over the nation and marched in Washington, D.C., and in other major U.S. cities on March 24, 2018. They marched in 800 venues around the world. Change will have to come from the Stoneman Douglas students who drove to Tallahassee, the students who participated in the national walkout, the teens who wrote *The New York Times* editorial, those who appeared on *60 Minutes* and MSNBC, and those who marched on March 24, 2018. It will never come if we rely on the Washington politicians, most of whom were out of town—if not out to lunch—when the young people marched in Washington, D.C.

Throughout, the Stoneman Douglas students not only comported themselves with class, but they revealed themselves to be young adults and genuine Americans. They point the way forward. Their passion reminds us of the drive for civil rights led by Dr. Martin Luther King, Jr. and of the young people who brought the Vietnam War to an end.

The gentleman from Parkland who told President Trump that he was pissed had a God-given right to be pissed. We should all be pissed. He and his wife conceived and brought their daughter into the world. They nurtured her, read books to her, hugged her, and comforted her when she needed it. They watched her and her friends grow up. They looked forward to graduation, possibly college, marriage, and grandchildren. Then, in a blinding flash it was all swept away. It could have been any one of us. His daughter is one of so many cruelly taken from us by mindless gun violence. The nation should stand shoulder-to-shoulder with that bereaved father and his family. All of us, including those who pursue gun rights, should. After the meeting in Parkland, President Trump said that had he been present at the time of the shooting, he would have charged the gunman even if he had no weapon. It is fair to ask the President, if you truly do have that kind of guts, why not step out front and back gun laws that remove military weapons from civilian life?

There have been school shootings where a student charged

the shooter. On April 30, 2019, a gunman shot and killed one student and wounded four others in a classroom at the University of North Carolina at Charlotte. When a 21-year-old student, Riley Howell, charged him the gunman shot Howell three times and killed him. The police said Howell's action prevented an even greater massacre.[8]

In a similar incident two students, Brendan Bialy and Kendrick Castillo, tackled a gunman at the STEM School in an English class at Highlands Ranch, Colorado on May 7, 2019. Highlands Ranch is near Columbine. Castillo was shot and killed. Two other students were killed and four others wounded in the incident. Bialy and Castillo were credited with stopping the massacre.[9]

Within days of the STEM School shooting, *The New York Times* reported that there had been 111 school shootings in the nation since 1970 and printed a map showing their location across the nation. It also printed a chart showing major school shootings, including:

School	Year	Deaths	Wounded
New York High School	1974	4	11
Stockton, California elementary school	1989	6	29
High school in Olivehurst, California	1992	4	10
Arkansas Middle School	1998	4	
Columbine High School, Colorado	1999	15	21
Santana High School outside San Diego	2001	2	13
West Nickel Mines, Pennsylvania, Amish elementary school	2006	5	
Sandy Hook elementary school, Connecticut	2012	28	2
Benton, Kentucky high school	2018	2	18
Santa Fe, New Mexico high school	2018	10	13
Parkland, Florida	2018	19	17 [10]

President Trump's comments that school shootings result from mental health issues do contain a measure of truth, but they should not be used as a ploy to steer debate away from military assault weapons. The shooters at Columbine, Virginia Tech, Sandy Hook, and Stoneman Douglas exhibited serious antisocial behavior. They were loners with similar social profiles. The federal government should develop programs and provide funds and programs to help young people with such issues. Our schools need improved and expanded services to help those who fall through the cracks. To paraphrase Edwin Markham's epigram, "Outwitted," our schools need to draw a circle that takes them in.[11]

Students deal with stress daily: maintaining grades to get into college, trying to be accepted, and handling social rejection. Rejected kids become loners. As sociologist William Isaac Thomas theorized, all kids, like the rest of us, wish for new experiences, security, recognition, and response.[12] Having more professionals on K-12 staffs to reach out to kids with social or mental issues will not solve all their problems, but it will give the kids someone they can talk to and help when they need it. Nor will it solve all the nation's gun problems, but it could help avoid some of the carnage.

After Stoneman Douglas, a sign that things may be changing came when Dick's Sporting Goods announced they would no longer sell assault rifles. Several major retailers announced they would no longer sell guns to persons under 21. This precipitated a lawsuit in Oregon by a 20-old man claiming Dick's and Walmart discriminated against him because they refused to sell him a rifle. Oregon law allows the sale of rifles and shotguns to 18-year-olds.[13] The American Federation of Teachers on April 19, 2018, notified Wells Fargo that it was dropping the bank as a recommended mortgage lender for its 1.7 million members for rejecting the union's call to cut ties with or impose restrictions on firearms-related businesses.[14] At its annual meeting on June 12, 2018, in Chicago, the American Medical Association recognized gun violence to be as menacing as infectious diseases and moved for a ban on assault weapons and opposed arming teachers.[15] On September 3, 2019, one month following the massacre at a Walmart store in El Paso, Texas, Walmart announced that it would stop selling ammunition that can be used in military assault rifles, would discourage customers from openly carrying guns in its stores, and would call on Congress to increase back-ground checks and consider a new assault rifle ban.[16]

While these current events offer hope, don't let that fool you. Within three months of Stoneman Douglas, Congress had re-sumed its efforts to bottle up any new laws, and the NRA held its annual conference at the convention center in Dallas, Texas, on the weekend of May 5, 2018. An estimated 80,000 NRA members attended. While addressing the conference President Trump reportedly stated, "Your Second Amendment rights are under siege, but they will never, ever be under siege as long as I am your President."[17]

That statement shattered any hope arising out of the Florida listening session that he would back the Stoneman Douglas students in their mission to get some new laws passed. Vice President Mike Pence in his address to the NRA reportedly stated to the assembled membership, "The quickest way to stop a bad guy with a gun is a good guy with a gun."[18] News reports, however, stated no guns were allowed at the NRA convention. If true, what does *that* tell us?

CHAPTER **10**

Terrorism and Hate Crimes

For all who draw the sword will die by the sword.
—*MATTHEW 26:52*

Returning violence for violence multiplies violence, adding deeper darkness to a night already devoid of stars.
—*Martin Luther King, Jr.*

Increasingly deadly acts of terrorism have been committed across our nation, making it imperative that firearms and explosives be kept out of the hands of terrorist groups and vigilantists. The victims of the incidents examined below were like the canaries that died in coalmines. They, along with many other incidents of gun violence, warned us of the risks we face from firearms and explosive devices acquired by terrorists, vigilantes, and others unfit to have them. We didn't heed the warnings from the many cages filled with dead canaries.

In August 1992, FBI agents and U.S. Marshals engaged in an 11-day standoff with white separatist Randy Weaver and his family at Ruby Ridge in Boundary County, Idaho. On the second day an FBI sharpshooter wounded Randy Weaver and Kevin Harrison, and killed Weaver's wife, Vicki. In the ensuing gun battle, U.S. Marshal Michael Degan was shot and killed.

On February 28, 1993, ATF agents arrived at the Mount Carmel Center, a ranch belonging to the Branch Davidian religious sect in Waco, Texas, led by David Koresh. The Branch Davidians had assembled an "army of God" and stockpiled weapons in preparation for the apocalypse. When the ATF agents tried to execute a search warrant, gunfire broke out. Four ATF agents and six Branch Davidians died. A siege of the compound lasted until April 19, 1993, when a fire erupted at the compound. Seventy-six Branch Davidians died in the fire.

On April 19, 1995, Timothy McVeigh and Terry Nichols set off a 5,000 pound truck bomb they had assembled using fertilizers and fuel oil outside of the Alfred P. Murrah Federal Building in Oklahoma City. At least 168 people died and more than 680 others were injured. Something like 258 other buildings in the area were destroyed, set on fire, or damaged by the blast. McVeigh and Nichols were alleged to be motivated by a dislike of the federal government and unhappiness over Ruby Ridge and the Branch Davidian incidents.[1]

On September 11, 2001, foreign terrorists skyjacked four jet airplanes, flew two of them into the twin towers of the World Trade Center in New York City destroying both towers, killing over 3,000 persons and inflicting grievous injuries upon thousands of others. The third jet was crashed into the Pentagon in Washington, D.C., and the fourth, believed to be targeting the White House, was crashed in a field in Pennsylvania.

During the annual Boston Marathon on April 15, 2013, two homemade pressure cooker bombs exploded 12 seconds apart at the finish line, killing three people and injuring over 260 others, including 16 who lost limbs. The FBI identified the bombers to be two brothers, Dzhokhar Tsarnaev and Tamerlan Tsarnaev, who were motivated by extremist Islamic beliefs and the wars in Iraq and Afghanistan.[2]

On December 3, 2015, Syed Farook and his wife, Tashfeen Malik—who had pledged allegiance to the terrorist group ISIS—shot and killed 14 people and wounded 17 others attending a holiday party at the Inland Regional Center, a social services center for disabled adults, in San Bernardino, California.[3] Their weapons included a Smith & Wesson M&P .223 caliber assault rifle, a DPMS Panther Arms .223 caliber assault rifle, and pipe bombs.[4] Both died in a shootout with police later that same day.

On April 18, 2017, another shooting spree occurred near the site of earlier mass shootings in Fresno, California. Kori Ali Muhammad a.k.a. Black Jesus, a 29-year-old homeless man who had an arrest record, fatally shot a passenger in a utility truck with a revolver and then walked for several blocks firing at people on the sidewalk and in a parking lot, killing two. Muhammad fired 16 bullets in a few minutes and reloaded once. All the victims were white. The police investigated whether it was a hate crime and whether Muhammad was tied to other gunshot victims and terrorist groups.[5]

During the week of October 21, 2018, 12 improvised bombs were sent through the U.S. mail addressed to Democrats including President Barak Obama, Vice President Joe Biden, Secretary of State Hillary Clinton, former officials of the United States appointed by Democrats, two U.S. senators, a congresswoman, and Democratic donors and supporters. None of the bombs exploded, and some were later discovered to be incapable of detonation. Following a swift FBI and state police investigation, the alleged perpetrator, Cesar Sayoc, Jr., was arrested in Florida. Sayoc was reported to be an avid supporter of President Trump.[6] Perhaps as some claim, the alleged mail bomber was only trying to send a message. If so the message is clear. There are those among us who will use explosive devices, death, destruction, and injury to send a political message.

On October 29, 2018, the mail bomb story was driven off the front pages. A gunman armed with an automatic rifle and three pistols fired on Jewish worshipers during Sabbath services at the Tree of Life Synagogue in Pittsburgh. He killed 11 family members and wounded six more, including four police officers. Those who died ranged in age from 54 to 97. The alleged perpetrator, Robert Bowers, had a history of posting anti-Semitic messages online. The FBI declared it a hate crime and took over prosecution of the case.[7]

Terrorism exploded again across the news media on August 3, 2019, when Patrick Crusius, a 21-year-old, shot 22 people dead and wounded 24 others at a Walmart store in El Paso, Texas. He came armed with an AK-47-style assault rifle and extra magazines. A witness said Crusius appeared to target Hispanics. He had posted a white nationalist, anti-immigrant manifesto against immigration online shortly before. The FBI is investigating it as domestic terrorism and a hate crime.[8]

The New York Times reported in November of 2019 that according to the annual FBI report for 2018, there were 7,120 incidents classified as hate crimes reported by law officers within the United States during 2018. This represented a 16-year high in crimes motivated by bias or prejudice. The article noted that physical assaults accounted for 61 percent of these crimes and that the crimes were committed against a wide range of racial and ethnic groups including African Americans, Latinos, Muslims, Arab-Americans, and Jewish people. The article reported that Jonathan Greenblatt, chief executive of the Anti-Defamation League, stated, "The surge of attacks on the Jewish community, in large cities like New York and in smaller cities like Pittsburgh and Poway, really has no precedent."[9]

In what police described as an anti-Semitic hate crime and an act of domestic terrorism four people including a police officer and the two assailants were killed at a kosher market operated by a Hasidic Jewish family in Jersey City, New Jersey, on Tuesday, December 10, 2019.[10]

Firearms were not involved in the terrorist bombing of the Murrah Building, on 9/11, at the Boston Marathon, or in the 2018 mail bomb attacks. But those incidents demonstrate that there are domestic and foreign terrorists among us who pose a grave threat to all of us, and that they *will* reach for whatever weapons are at hand.

When the Supreme Court elevated the private right to bear arms to the level of a constitutionally protected right in 2008, it confirmed that guns will be part of civilian life for the foreseeable future. So where do we go from here? What fountainheads of law can provide a lawful basis for regulation? To examine that issue, the next two chapters explore Congressional power to regulate guns and to bring the gun violence chronicled above under common sense control.

CHAPTER 11

Congress's Commerce Power under the Constitution

Congress was designed by the Founding Fathers to move slowly, precisely to avoid the sudden panic of a one-week solution that becomes a 20-year mess.
—*Newt Gingrich*

Among its enumerated powers in Article I Section 8 of the Constitution, Congress has power to regulate commerce with other countries, among the states, and with Indian tribes. Firearms and ammunition for them are interstate commerce commodities. Congress's Article I power to regulate interstate commerce includes the authority to remove obstacles to interstate commerce and to even regulate intrastate commerce that substantially affects interstate commerce.

Congress's efforts to exercise its Article I commerce power during the last century have repeatedly clashed with classic state police power. Litigation arising out of that clash produced a whole body of case law dealing with the reach of the Commerce Clause. The courts used parts of those decisions to strike down some legislation, but Congress retains substantial power under the Commerce Clause to regulate firearms and has used that power to require that importers, manufacturers, and dealers in firearms be licensed. It also forbade the sale of certain types of weapons such as sawed-off shotguns, machine guns, and for a while, semi-automatic assault weapons in interstate commerce.[1] The Brady Act, which requires background checks, is also part of the federal statutory scheme.[2]

There are limits to using the Commerce Clause. Congress

provided in the Gun-Free School Zones Act of 1990 that it was a federal offense "for any individual knowingly to possess a firearm at a place that the individual knows, or has reasonable cause to believe, is a school zone."[3] Congress's power to adopt the Gun-Free School Zones Act[4] came before the Supreme Court in *United States v. Lopez.*[5]

In March 1992, 12th-grade student Alfonso Lopez arrived at Edison High School in San Antonio, Texas, carrying a concealed .38 caliber handgun with five bullets. Acting on an anonymous tip, school officials confronted Lopez and he was subsequently charged under Texas law with firearm possession on school premises and convicted of violating the federal statute. The Fifth Circuit Court of Appeals[6] reversed the conviction. On appeal the Supreme Court held that the Act exceeded Congress's power under the Commerce Clause.

In his *Lopez* opinion, Chief Justice Rehnquist reviewed the Supreme Court's prior commerce cases and drew from them "three broad categories of activity" Congress could regulate under its commerce power:[7]

- the use of the channels of interstate commerce
- protecting the instrumentalities of interstate commerce or persons or things in interstate commerce, even though the threat may come only from intrastate activities
- those activities that substantially affect interstate commerce

Rehnquist rejected the first two of his tests and concluded that to be within the area that Congress may regulate under the Commerce Clause, gun-free school zones must affect or substantially affect interstate commerce. He found they did not.

Most of the commerce power cases involved economic or commercial interests like chicken farming and wheat farming, not public safety. When it decided *Lopez*, the Court refused to extend what it perceived to be a too-liberal interpretation of Congress's commerce power and concluded that carrying a handgun into a public school could not be regulated under the clause because it was a purely local matter that had no impact on interstate commerce. If Congress cannot use its commerce power to protect students in a local school, then the issue becomes whether it can use that power to prevent the carriage of firearms into *any* public buildings or even on city streets. Many public institutions, however, are themselves in commerce.

The Commerce Clause is the preferred method Congress has used to enact gun legislation. That clause certainly provides Congress ample power to regulate the carriage and use of guns in the instrumentalities of interstate commerce such as railways, airlines, and public places. It also gives it power to regulate guns and ammunition that move or are sold in interstate commerce and power to free that commerce from acts of violence that might disrupt it. After *Lopez* was decided, the Gun-Free School Zones Act was amended to provide that firearms that had moved in interstate commerce could be excluded from school zones. *Lopez* teaches, however, that Congress, in controlling the use of firearms, could not regulate purely local activities.[8]

In *Jay Printz v. United States*,[9] the Supreme Court also held that Congress could not commandeer local sheriffs or police offices to perform background checks to enforce the Brady Act. The Court noted that if local officials volunteered to perform background checks, there would not have been a breach of federal-state sovereignty. Congress could exploit that distinction and incorporate into a federal uniform law provisions for joint federal-state enforcement on a consensual basis. With strict protocols to protect privacy, oversight of information access, and secure data storage, they could collect relevant background data and assist in maintaining a database for issuing licenses.[10]

Lopez and *Printz* pose serious obstacles to uniform national regulation at the local level, but they also teach that regulation should be directed at the guns themselves. If Congress lacks power under the Commerce Clause to impose regulations on local school districts because they are not deemed to be in commerce, then it must use its powers to control the guns and ammunition that move in or impact interstate commerce. It can use that power to determine who may carry weapons, what weapons they may carry, and in many cases where they may carry them.

Other provisions of the Constitution permit exertion of federal power into local areas even if the Commerce Clause does not, and they also suggest that there may be areas for a joint federal-state regulatory scheme on a consensual basis. The commerce power and Congress's power to tax as used to support the 1934 Act, will not suffice to place existing military assault weapons and other highly dangerous weapons already privately held under control. Other sources of congressional power must be explored to deal with that problem.

CHAPTER 12

Congress's Militia Power under the Constitution

I ask, sir, what is the militia? It is the whole people except for a few public officials.
—George Mason

The use of Congress's militia powers may sound at first blush like a bizarre, novel idea, but nothing in the *Heller* or *McDonald* opinions precludes a law that regulates firearms purchased or carried as part of the militia. If Supreme Court commerce decisions do not permit use of the Commerce Clause to control purely local activity, then why not explore other avenues of regulating military assault weapons? Consider that the Second Amendment uses the term "well regulated" in describing the militia.

The militia is not new or novel. It was used to win the American Revolution. Under existing Supreme Court case law, every citizen has a duty to serve in the United States military or a state militia when called upon by the authorities. Congress has power "to provide for calling forth the militia to execute the laws of the Union, suppress insurrections and repel invasions; to provide for organizing, arming, and disciplining the Militia, and for governing such part of them as may be employed in the service of the United States, reserving to the states respectively, the appointment of the officers, and the authority of training the militia according to the discipline prescribed by Congress."[1]

If it so wished Congress could fully employ its militia powers and declare a national emergency resulting from the staggering loss of human life and threat to society caused by the deployment of military assault weapons within our civilian population. It could require that all persons who are now licensed or wish to be permitted to own and carry military assault firearms enlist in state units of the National Guard—which has supplanted the militia—as a condition of holding, carrying, or using military assault weapons. This would subject all military assault weapons as defined by Congress and now held by private citizens to the regulations and commands of the National Guard. Under current federal statutes Congress could use the National Guard to impound military assault weapons if found in the possession of unauthorized persons or persons unfit to have them. Such a requirement would not ban the ownership or carriage of firearms for self-defense, hunting, or recreation.

Hamilton et al. v. Regents of the University of California[2] held that both federal and state governments owes a duty to the people within its jurisdiction to provide adequate military and police strength to maintain peace and order and to assure the just enforcement of law, and that every citizen owe a reciprocal duty, according to their capacity, to support and defend government against all enemies.[3]

In October 1933 the minor plaintiffs in *Hamilton* became students at the University of California, a land grant college. The university required that all able-bodied male students who were citizens of the United States enroll in military science and tactics courses. The program, run through a Reserve Officers Training Corps as an integral part of the United States military establishment, though not connected to the United States War Department, included instruction in rifle marksmanship, scouting and patrolling, drill and command, combat principles, and automatic rifles. The War Department furnished arms, equipment, and uniforms. Plaintiffs petitioned the university for exemption from participation based upon their religious and conscientious objections to war and military training. Their petition was denied.

Congress had provided for land grant colleges through the Morrill Act.[4] That act provided that acceptance of benefits from the Act required that at least one of a recipient school's colleges teach military tactics.[5] In the course of carrying out the Morrill Act, California passed a law that any state resident 14 years and older would receive instruction and discipline in military tactics. The Regents—the governing body of the University of California system—later implemented an order requiring completion of specific courses in military science.

The *Hamilton* plaintiffs lost in the lower courts but appealed to the Supreme Court where they asked that California's constitution, organic act, and the Regents' order, in so far as they imposed compulsory military training, be held repugnant to the privileges and immunities clause of the Fourteenth Amendment, the due process clause of that amendment, and the Kellogg-Briand Peace Pact or Pact of Paris.[6]

Citing *State v. Holm,*[7] *State v. Johnson,*[8] and the Constitution,[9] the Court said that every state has authority to train its able-bodied male citizens of suitable age to develop fitness to serve in the United States Army or a state militia. They may be called forth by federal authority to execute the laws of the Union, suppress insurrection, or repel invasion. The Court added that the state, in order to train its citizens for these purposes, may avail itself of the services of officers and equipment belonging to the United States military establishment. The Court said that so long as its actions were within the state's retained powers, not inconsistent with any exertion of the authority of the national government, and transgressed no right safeguarded to the citizen by the federal Constitution, the state would be the sole judge of the means to be employed and the amount of training exacted for the effective accomplishment of these ends.

In response to the appellants' contention that enforcement of the order prescribing instruction in military science and tactics abridged privileges and immunities given them by the first clause of the Fourteenth Amendment and deprived them of the liberty safeguarded by the second clause of that amendment, the Court said that the privileges and immunities protected under that amendment are only those belonging to citizens of the United States as distinguished from citizens of the states.

The Court said that the privilege of attending the university as a student did not arise from federal sources but was given by the state and so was not a Fourteenth Amendment protected privilege. The immunity the students claimed—to be exempted from the Regents' mandated military training—couldn't be distinguished from the claim that the order deprived plaintiffs of their liberty. The Court held that if the Regents' order was not repugnant to the due process clause, it did not violate the plaintiffs' privileges and immunities and the only question before it, the Court said, was whether plaintiffs' liberty had been infringed.

In *Hamilton*, the Court said that the privilege of even native-born conscientious objectors to avoid bearing arms comes not from the Constitution, but from acts of Congress which may grant or withhold the exemption as in its wisdom it sees fit. Congress's war powers include the power to compel the armed service of any citizen in the land, without regard to his objections or his views on the justice or morality of the particular war or of war in general. In *Jacobson v. Massachusetts*,[10] where the Court upheld a state compulsory vaccination law, it said that a citizen, "may be compelled, by force if need be, against his will and without regard to his personal wishes or his pecuniary interests or even his religious or political convictions, to take his place in the ranks of the army of his country, and risk the chance of being shot down in its defense."

Justice Benjamin N. Cardozo, joined by Justices Louis Brandeis and Harlan F. Stone, concurred in *Hamilton*. Justice Cardozo pointed out that when Quakers and other conscientious objectors were exempted from military service as an act of grace, the exemption in many instances was coupled with a condition that they supply the Army with a substitute or with the money necessary to hire one. So existing precedent establishes that under the Constitution all citizens who are of age are members of the militia and subject to such regulation as set by Congress, which can direct under its militia powers that *military assault weapons* may only be possessed or carried by persons who have been "called forth to execute the laws of the union" and have become members of the active militia or a state National Guard unit. Under its militia powers, Congress can discipline those in the militia with respect to the guns and ammunition they may possess, where they may carry them, and the manner in which they shall house and use such firearms. It's entirely sensible to place military weapons under military control.

By law, state National Guard units can now execute the laws of the Union. According to the Militia Act of 1903,[11] militia refers primarily to two groups: the organized militia consisting of state militia forces (National Guard and Naval Militia) and an unorganized militia consisting of the reserve militia, which consists of every able-bodied citizen between 18 and 45 years old who is not a member of the National Guard or Naval Militia.[12]

It seems clear that in its *Heller* decision the Supreme Court recognized that firearms and explosive devices *classified as military weapons* can be well-regulated by Congress. So it's appropriate that the thousands of privately-owned military assault weapons like the AR-15 now in civilian hands be placed under the command of military officers by enacting a uniform national law. Under Article I, Section 8 of the Constitution, existing National Guard units in the several states, the District of Columbia, and U.S. territories could be called forth to regulate the ownership, storage, and carriage of such weapons pursuant to the Act of 1903 and United States military laws governing the National Guard.

In the National Defense Authorization Act for Fiscal Years 1990 and 1991,[13] Congress provided for distribution of military assault weapons and other military surplus gear by duly constituted and licensed auxiliary state and municipal police forces under the control of state and municipal governments. The Law Enforcement Support Office (LESO)[14] implements the 1033 program for law enforcement agencies to acquire military surplus property to assist in their arrest and apprehension mission. It provides a lawful opportunity for qualified trained personnel to carry and use military assault firearms. It would provide a means to require that those owning these weapons train and develop skills in their safe handling and storage. It could also provide a procedure for the federal government to buy back military assault weapons now held by civilians and use them for military or police purposes.

Serving in the National Guard or auxiliary police forces, good guys (and women) with guns could protect schools and other public places in addition to their deployments in areas struck by natural disasters, civil unrest, armed insurrections, or acts of terrorism. The federal and state governments can share the National Guard, set membership standards, require periodic training as the Military Reserves do, and order deployment as they did in response to the 9/11 attacks and 1999 rioting during the Seattle World Trade Organization talks.[15]

In short, use of Congress's power to call forth and regulate the militia (National Guard) is not a far-fetched idea. The Constitution permits it, and it is a good fit with the existing need to well-regulate military assault weapons held by unregulated civilians and devote them to lawful military and police uses. However, the overriding issue remains: is it possible to get any kind of regulation done in the existing political climate? The next chapter examines that problem.

13

The Gun Lobby and *Citizens United*

All contributions by corporations to any political committee or for any political purpose should be forbidden by law.
—*Theodore Roosevelt*

Finance is a gun. Politics is knowing when to pull the trigger.
—*Mario Puzo*

Recent polls indicate that the number of persons favoring more stringent gun controls is growing. A Quinnipiac University Poll[1] taken February 20, 2018, found that Americans support stricter gun laws 66 percent to 31 percent. A Gallup Poll[2] taken October 5–11, 2017, showed 60 percent of respondents favor stricter gun control laws, 33 percent responded *keep as now*, and 5 percent responded *less strict*. The Gallup Poll also indicated that the percentage of respondents favoring a law making it illegal to manufacture, sell, or possess semiautomatic assault rifles rose from 36 percent in October 2016 to 48 percent in October 2017 and that the percentage against dropped from 61 percent in 2016 to 49 percent in 2017. A poll taken by *Business Insider* following the shooting at Stoneman Douglas on February 14, 2018, found that 70 percent of Americans supported stricter laws for assault weapons.[3]

Bottom line, the electorate wants common sense gun laws, *Heller* does not block them and still we don't have them. Why not?

Congress has ample power to legislate. The crux of the problem is that Congress will not act. The reason is money—campaign money. Sensible gun regulation will never come into being unless the gun lobby's stranglehold on our politicians is broken. Look at the record.

Consider that since 1968, while gun deaths, mass murder, terrorism and devastating injuries escalated, we have had two new gun control laws: the Violent Crime Act and Enforcement Act of 1994 which expired in 2004 and the Brady Handgun Violence Prevention Act of 1993. The Protection of Lawful Commerce in Arms of Act of 2005 that granted immunity from civil liability to gun manufacturers and dealers, and the statute that prevented the Centers for Disease Control from spending public money on researching gunshot injuries,[4] freed guns from regulation instead of regulating them.

Neither the 1968 act nor the 1994 act banned the thousands of machine guns, semiautomatics, large capacity magazines, nor bump stocks[5] held by gun owners prior to the effective dates of those acts. Despite over 2,000 bills introduced since 1968, Congress has failed to enact any effective regulation to cover all points of sale and transfer.[6] Gun rights advocates, gun manufacturers, and their lobbyists expect the nation to lay the 1.4 million victims of gun violence during the last half century[7] as a sacrifice on the altar of the Second Amendment. *Guns don't kill, people do, good guys with a gun, and cold dead hands,* are trotted out to combat even the most innocuous proposals. If the gun rights people adamantly stand their ground with respect to semiautomatic firearms and open carry, the ultimate victims will be the rule of law and the Constitution.

A. The NRA

U.S. Senator Marco Rubio (R-Florida) was interviewed on television following the horrific events at Stoneman Douglas. Senator Rubio comes across as a responsible, reasonable senator, and to his credit he had the guts to show up during a question and answer session with the President and later for questions. But when asked several times to reconsider accepting campaign contributions from the NRA, he responded that his positions on gun rights were his personal positions arrived at on his own. He said that if others believed in his positions and wished to donate to his campaigns it was their choice. If true, that can only mean that Senator Rubio adopted and maintains his views on gun rights untainted by the interest of any lobbyists. That he, on his own, sincerely believes in the unregulated manufacture and sale of military assault weapons now in the civilian gun markets; that he believes it is sound national policy to place these weapons into the hands of unregulated civilians knowing it is inevitable that massacres *will* continue.[8]

The NRA participates in political campaigns through its lobbying arm, the Institute for Legislative Action (NRA-ILA) and the NRA Political Victory Fund (PVF), its political action committee managed by NRA-ILA. According to a Federal Election Commission (FEC) report available on the internet, the NRA-ILA dispersed $852,572.76 and the PVF dispersed $61,950.64 to pay expenses in support of Senator Rubio's campaigns for the 2016 Republican nomination for President and later for the Senate seat he holds now. The Appendix, compiled from data that the FEC published on the internet, shows expenses paid by the NRA's committees supporting or opposing candidates for national office during the 2016 election cycle. The NRA doesn't lay out the kind of money shown in the Appendix for politicians given low marks. It strains credulity beyond the breaking point to assert that support of this magnitude will not influence Senator Rubio's voting record as a Senator. It just doesn't wash.

But that is the position candidates find themselves in under our campaign contribution laws. Senator Rubio is just an example. Many of his colleagues in Congress, the Oval Office, and state houses would answer the same as he did. After Las Vegas, Sutherland Springs, and Stoneman Douglas, we would expect bipartisan proposals for controls on military assault weapons from our elected representatives. If they have none, that speaks for itself. When the history of political campaign finance is laid beside our history with gun violence and Congress's feeble efforts to control it, a wholly different story from the one espoused by Senator Rubio and his colleagues emerges.

The NRA is an American nonprofit organization that advocates for gun rights. The NRA doesn't release membership figures, but its estimated five million members account for less than 10 percent of the gun-owning population.[9] In 1871 Civil War veterans George Wood Wingate, a lawyer, and William Conant Church, a former *New York Times* reporter, founded the NRA to promote rifle marksmanship, not gun rights.[10] Originally, the NRA taught firearms competency and safety and offered instructional programs for civilians and law enforcement.

The NRA has a tax-exempt nonprofit organization status under §501(c) (4) of the Internal Revenue Code. That means the Internal Revenue Service considers it a social welfare organization, which under the tax code must not be organized for profit and must be operated exclusively to promote social welfare. "The promotion of social welfare does not include direct or indirect participation or intervention in political campaigns on behalf of or in opposition to any candidate for public office. However, a section 501(c) (4) social welfare organization may engage in some political activities, so long as that is not its primary activity."[11]

The NRA created a Legislative Affairs Division following enactment of the National Firearms Act of 1934. The *Washington Post* reports that Karl Frederick, the president of the NRA in 1934, testified during Congressional hearings for the 1934 Act: "I have never believed in the general practice of carrying weapons. I seldom carry one . . . I do not believe in the general promiscuous toting of guns. I think it should be sharply restricted and only under licenses."[12]

But the NRA's mission changed. According to the Association's by-laws, its purpose and objective now is to ". . . to protect and defend the Constitution of the United States, especially with reference to the inalienable right of the individual American citizen guaranteed by such Constitution to acquire, possess, collect, exhibit, transport, carry, transfer ownership of, and enjoy the right to use arms." Today the NRA zealously promotes that mission.

The NRA supported most provisions of the Gun Control Act of 1968 but blocked a mandate for a national gun registry.[13] That is when the change began to manifest. On May 21, 1977, a caucus of gun rights radicals took over the NRA's annual meeting, wearing orange-blaze hunting caps. After the so-called "revolt at Cincinnati",[14] the NRA began to focus on political issues. Neal Knox was elected executive director and head of the NRA-ILA. In 1994 the NRA unsuccessfully opposed the federal assault weapons ban but lobbied for and got that Act's 2004 sunset date. By 1998 the NRA's PVF was reported to be one of the biggest spenders in Congressional elections. In 2004 the NRA opposed renewal of the assault weapons ban of 1994 which then expired. In 2005, it backed the

Protection of Lawful Commerce in Arms Act (discussed in Chapter 5 above) that shielded manufacturers and dealers from negligence liability if crimes were committed with their products.[15] *That* bill was voted into law.

Today the NRA is a single-issue organization focusing on Second Amendment issues. Its PVF grades candidates for public office based on their positions on gun rights. A candidate assigned an A+ rating has "not only an excellent voting record on all critical NRA issues, but who has also made a vigorous effort to promote and defend the Second Amendment."[16]

Candidates boast about high NRA ratings and use them as dog whistles during their campaigns. The NRA reportedly spent $40 million in the 2008 presidential campaign opposing the election of Barack Obama.[17] Following the mass shootings at Aurora, Colorado, and Sandy Hook, Connecticut, John Morse and Angela Giron, state senators in Colorado, helped the Colorado legislature pass expanded background checks and ammunition magazine capacity limits. The NRA's committees reportedly spent over $500,000 in an election that recalled both Morse and Giron.[18]

It's not the only gun rights lobby, but it's the most powerful and reported to be one of the top three influential lobbying groups in Washington, D.C. The NRA's activities include the payment of expenses to support candidates and to oppose others through its committees, direct campaign donations, and various activities that some see as benefiting the firearms and ammunition industry. The NRA also helps its members to locate an NRA Election Volunteer Coordinator for their area and to register voters. The NRA, in short, participates in candidate election campaigns. The NRA also appears amicus in litigation to resist gun control laws as it did in the *McDonald* case. It has similarly appeared to defend gun manufacturers from liability. The Sandy Hook families sued Remington, a gun manufacturer that had acquired the rights to manufacture the Bushmaster used at Sandy Hook, claiming the defendant sold the weapon by advertising that the weapon provided *combat dominance*. Remington filed for bankruptcy reorganization and on motion the local court stayed the families' lawsuit until Remington emerged from bankruptcy. When the families appealed the stay order to the Connecticut Supreme Court, the NRA filed as an amicus claiming the lawsuit stood to eviscerate Remington's legal protection from litigation.[19]

B. NRA Money

Pinning down total amounts received and contributions made by the NRA and its several lobbying and fundraising committees to political candidates is a formidable task. *The Hill*, a publication that investigates political and financial aspects of Congress, the Administration, lobbying and campaigns, reports that the NRA received $336.7 million in revenue during 2015, including $165.7 million from membership dues.[20] According to *The Hill* the gross receipts for the NRA Foundation, which raises funds to help support "a wide range of firearms-related public interest activities," during 2015 totaled $101.16 million. The NRA Civil Rights Defense Fund received $1.58 million in 2015 to fund cases "involving significant legal issues relating to the right to keep and bear arms."[21] The PVF received $21.6 million in donations in the 2016 election cycle.

The Hill also reports the NRA's spending for Donald Trump's presidential campaign in 2016 totaled $31,194,646 when you include monies paid for expenses to support Donald Trump and those to oppose Hillary Clinton. That same calculation performed using data drawn from the Federal Election Report for the 2016 election, described above, totals $42,364,305. Election expense reports filed with the FEC indicate that in 2016 the NRA's lobbying and political action arms paid out $23,858,077 to oppose Hillary Clinton's bid to become president, and $18,506,328 to support that of Donald Trump.

The Hill report shows the following outside spending for other candidates in the 2016 election:[22]

Sen. Richard Burr (R-N.C.)	$6,297,551
Sen. Marco Rubio (R-Fla.)	$3,298,405
Sen. Roy Blunt (R-Mo.)	$3,105,294
Sen. Todd Young (R-Ind.)	$2,888,132
Former Rep. Joe Heck (R-Nev.)	$2,529,305
Sen. Rob Portman (R-Ohio)	$2,319,755
Sen. Ron Johnson (AR-Wis.)	$650,745
Rep. Lloyd Smucker (R-Pa.)	$215,786
Sen. Richard Shelby (R-Ala.)	$167,411

The Hill numbers are significantly higher than FEC-published numbers, described above, that list election expenses paid by the NRA's committees during 2016. For example, the total in the Appendix for Richard Burr is $514,184, and for Marco Rubio $914,522. No explanation for this difference has been found. *The Hill* report also states that according to a spreadsheet compiled by the Center for Responsive Politics, the NRA spent $66 million electing 249 members of Congress and 54 senators as well as defeating their opponents. The latter calculation includes amounts spent over the lawmakers' careers dating back to 1989 when you include donations, independent expenditures from the NRA's PACs, and money directly from NRA members.

The Hill report states, "The amount the NRA and its affiliates spent on independent expenditures in the 2016 election cycle, according to FEC records," was more than $54 million. The Appendix, compiled from data published on the Internet by the FEC, shows that amount to be $66,325,710 for those candidates listed when expenses to both support and oppose candidates are added together. While reports of the NRA's committees' total spending on behalf of political candidates are inconsistent, it is clear that the NRA through its committees spends substantial sums to help candidates it has given high marks and to oppose those it does not.

According to Snopes.com, the urban legends and fact checking site, some critics have challenged the NRA's status as a social welfare organization, claiming that it spends less time and money providing a genuine service to the public than it does on funding political campaigns and for political lobbying.[23] The NRA responded to Snopes.com that the NRA's legislative lobbying is textbook social welfare activity, and that case law has established that "occasional private financial benefits resulting incidentally from a nonprofit group's activities are allowed."[24] When one examines all of the activities of the NRA, it is extremely difficult not to conclude that it has morphed from a social welfare organization into a vigorous political action group supporting the economic well-being of gun manufacturers and dealers.

This book does not seek to challenge the NRA's tax-exempt status, however. That issue is left to tax lawyers, accountants, and the IRS. The goal here is to demonstrate that the NRA's political activities, whether incidental or its main mission, have killed rational gun regulation. Gun Owners of America (GOA) is another 501(c) (4) nonprofit organization dedicated to defending the Second Amendment rights of gun owners. It claims over 1.5 million members;[25] other sources report its membership at 300,000.[26] According to the OpenSecrets.org database, GOA affiliates contributed over $1.485 million to candidates' campaigns from 1990 to 2018.[27] Gun rights organizations contributed $42,320,882 during 1990–2018 election cycles.[28] Top lobbying groups, including the NRA, National Shooting Sports Foundation, and National Association for Gun Rights, contributed $9.88 million just in 2017.[29]

C. Citizen Corporations

But the massive contributions that the NRA and the gun lobby inject into political campaigns don't tell the whole story. To respond to the position asserted by Senator Rubio and his colleagues, we have to step back a bit and examine all corporate campaign contributions. In one of the most far-reaching decisions it ever rendered, *Trustees of Dartmouth College v. Woodward*,[30] the Supreme Court found that the Charter of Dartmouth College, a private school, was a contract that the state of New Hampshire could not impair. The Court relied on Article I, Section 10 of the Constitution, which says, "No state shall . . . pass any . . . law . . . impairing the obligations of contracts."

Chief Justice Marshall wrote: "A corporation is an artificial being, invisible, intangible, and existing only in contemplation of law. Being the mere creature of law, it possesses only those properties which the charter of its creation confers upon it, either expressly or as incidental to its very existence. These are such as are supposed best calculated to effect the object for which it was created."[31]

The *Dartmouth College* decision settled the nature of public versus private charters and resulted in the rise of the American business corporation and the free enterprise system.[32] Both are laudable achievements. Today thousands of corporations are registered to sell their stocks on the New York Stock Exchange (NYSE), American Stock Exchange (AMEX), and National Association of Securities Dealers Automated Quotation System (NASDAQ). The amalgamated wealth controlled within the corporate world is unimaginably immense.

Long before the modern era of campaign contributions, the federal courts recognized that a business corporation was a "citizen" for purposes of Article III, Section 3 of the Constitution: that the judicial power of the United States extends to controversies arising between citizens of different states. Our federal courts routinely recognize that business corporations and labor unions are citizens of the states where they are incorporated or organized for purposes of diversity jurisdiction. Corporations and labor unions as citizens can sue and be sued in the federal courts.

But the courts have never held that a labor union or corporation enjoys all the rights of living flesh and blood people under the Constitution. Certainly, business corporations and labor unions can't vote or hold public office. But to what extent is a business corporation or a labor union a citizen that entitles it to participate in federal and state elections? Can they support candidates or issues with corporate or union funds, air electioneering television spots or internet videos, make robocalls, lobby elected officials, organize blocs of voters, spend "dark money"*, or retaliate against elected representatives who oppose their agenda? Equally important, can the amount of money they contribute to political campaigns be limited?

D. The First Amendment and Campaign Finance

Business corporations and unions have deep pockets—their resources dwarf that of the general electorate or the so-called man in the street. Add in the resources of their stockholders, officers, members, and supporters as well as their trade associations and lobbying groups. Recently our courts examined this issue as a question of freedom of speech under the First Amendment. But the issue is not only one of free speech. It threatens the validity of our elections, the fidelity of members of Congress and state legislatures, the even-handed execution of our laws, and the rule of law itself. It most assuredly impacts the raging debate over gun control.

The First Amendment provides that, "Congress shall make no law . . . abridging the freedom of speech." The Supreme Court held that the First Amendment applies to corporations in *First*

---

*Political spending meant to influence the decision of a voter where the donor is not disclosed and the source of the money is unknown. Depending upon the circumstances, Dark Money can refer to funds spent by a political nonprofit or a super PAC (political action committee). While super PACs are legally required to disclose their donors, they can accept unlimited contributions from political nonprofits and "shell" corporations who may not have disclosed their donors.

National Bank of Boston v. Bellotti.[33] But in a facial challenge heard in 2003—where the plaintiff argued that campaign regulation legislation is always unconstitutional and therefore void—the Supreme Court upheld limits on electioneering communications by corporations,[34] relying on its 1990 decision in *Austin v. Michigan Chamber of Commerce,*[35] which held that political speech may be banned based on the speaker's corporate identity. *Austin* recognized a governmental interest in "preventing the corrosive and distorting effects of immense aggregations of (corporate wealth) that have little or no correlation to the public's support for the corporation's political ideas."[36]

Recall again that while recent polls show broad public support for increased gun controls, Congress has passed no new gun laws.

The Bipartisan Campaign Reform Act of 2002[37] (BCRA) amended federal law to prohibit corporations and unions from using general treasury funds to make speech that is an electioneering communication or that expressly advocates the election or defeat of a candidate. The BCRA defined an *electioneering communication* to be "any broadcast, cable, or satellite communication (that) refers to a clearly identified candidate for public office," made within 30 days of a primary election.[38] The BCRA provided that corporations and unions could establish PACs for advocacy or electioneering communications purposes.[39]

E. *Citizens United*

In January 2008 Citizens United, a nonprofit corporation—not a PAC of a corporation—released a documentary, *Hillary*, that was critical of then-Senator Hillary Clinton, who was seeking the Democratic Party nomination for President of the United States. Citizens United intended to make *Hillary* available on cable television through video on demand within 30 days of primary elections and generated television ads promoting *Hillary* to run on broadcast and cable television. Citizens United filed a lawsuit in the Federal District Court for the District of Columbia arguing that sections of the BCRA were unconstitutional as applied to *Hillary* and the ads. A three-judge panel of the District Court denied injunctive relief and granted the FEC summary judgment.

In *Citizens United v. Federal Election Commission,* the Supreme Court refused to address the issues on narrower grounds and in a five–four decision ruled that the restrictions on corporate and union political contributions imposed by BCRA operated as a prior restraint on free speech in violation of the First Amendment.[40] It said the BCRA restrictions on corporate expenditures were an outright ban on speech. In short, *Austin*[41] was overruled. The Court held that *Austin* provided no basis for allowing the government to limit corporate independent expenditures. The Court also overruled the section in *McConnell*[42] that upheld BCRA's restrictions on independent corporate expenditures.

The Court in *Citizens United* said that laws burdening free speech, "are subject to strict scrutiny," and the Court must find that any such restriction "furthers a compelling interest and is narrowly tailored to achieve that interest."[43] Applying that rule, the Court held that First Amendment protections do not depend on the speaker's financial ability to engage in public discussion; however, the Court did uphold the disclaimer and disclosure requirements of the BCRA with respect to the advertisements publicizing *Hillary*. In upholding them the Court said, "Disclosure can be justified by a government interest in providing the electorate with information about election-related spending sources." Citizens was a nonprofit corporation so there was no need to announce a rule that applied to profit corporations, but that's what the Court did in *Citizens United*.

Four Justices dissented in *Citizens United*. Justice Stevens, citing his concurrence in *Austin,* wrote: "A referendum [*sic*] cannot owe a political debt to a corporation, seek to curry favor with a corporation, or fear the corporation's retaliation."[44]

Foreseeing the position we now find ourselves in with respect to campaign finance laws, Justice Stevens added:

- On numerous occasions we have recognized Congress's legitimate interest in preventing the money that is spent on elections from exerting an "undue influence on an officeholder's judgment" and from creating "the appearance of such influence," beyond the sphere of quid pro quo relationships. . . .

- Corruption operates along a spectrum and the majority's apparent belief that quid pro quo arrangements can be neatly demarcated from other improper influences does not accord with the theory or reality of politics. . . .[45]

– When private interests are seen to exert outsized control over officeholders solely on account of the money spent on (or withheld from) their campaigns, the result can depart so thoroughly "from what is pure or correct" . . . that it amounts to a subversion . . . of the electoral process. . . .[46]

– A democracy cannot function effectively when its constituent members believe laws are being bought and sold. . . .[47]

– The influx of unlimited corporate money into the electoral realm also creates new opportunities for the mirror image of quid pro quo deals: threats both explicit and implicit.[48]

Commercial corporations were developed to permit aggregations of capital far beyond that which sole proprietorships or partnerships can amass. They were granted limited liability by law to shield their shareholders from liability and to carry out their mission. A corporation's powers are those granted to it in its charter pursuant to the state law under which it was incorporated. They are creatures of the law. It is one thing for the Supreme Court to say a corporation has a right to speak on matters of political concern under the First Amendment. It is quite another to say that its right to speak includes a right to displace legitimate government. To allow the wealth of commercial corporations to take over our political system destroys the right of flesh-and-blood citizens to speak. It speaks so loudly it drowns out the voices of the people.

The Supreme Court's opinion in *Citizens United* critically impacts the debate on effective gun control. Substantial increases occurred in the amount of corporate funds expended for gun rights through direct contributions to candidates, soft money, dark money, and lobbying activities since *Citizens United* was decided in 2010.[49] The magnitude of dark money that gun manufacturers and dealers contribute to candidates may never be known. Now the issue is whether all that money is destroying government of the people, by the people, and for the people.

E. Other Court Decisions

In the 2014 case *McCutcheon vs. Federal Election Commission*,[50] the Court struck down (5 to 4) provisions of the Federal Election Campaign Act of 1971 (FECA) as amended by the BCRA. Those two laws had imposed limits on the amount of money a donor could contribute to a particular candidate or committee and an aggregate limit on the total amount of money a donor could contribute to several candidates or committees. The Court held that the aggregate limit violated the First Amendment but left the base limit for a particular candidate or committee in place.

Back in 1976 before BCRA was enacted, in *Buckley v. Valeo*[51] the Court had declared the FECA's independent expenditures ceiling to be a substantial and direct restriction on the ability of candidates, citizens, and associations to engage in protected political expression, "that the First Amendment could not tolerate." The *Buckley* Court expressly held, though, that the aggregate limit established by FECA for direct contributions to candidates or candidate committees did not violate the First Amendment. But as stated above, the *McCutcheon* Court ruled that the *Buckley* decision did not control it with respect to the aggregate limit on contributions to candidates or candidate committees established by the two acts.

Writing for the majority in *McCutcheon*, Chief Justice Roberts stated: "To require one person to contribute at lower levels than others because he wants to support more candidates or causes is to impose a special burden on broader participation in the democratic process.… The Government may not penalize an individual for robustly exercis[ing] his First Amendment rights."[52] When the dust settled the independent expenditures limit of FECA was struck down by *Buckley*, and the aggregate direct campaign contribution limit for particular candidates or committees was struck down in *McCutcheon*. Taken together the two decisions dismantled two separate laws that had been enacted by majority votes of the people's representatives in two separate Congresses to place limits on political campaign contributions. *McCutcheon* was decided by the vote of five justices. Had one justice voting with the majority shifted his vote, the decision in *McCutcheon* would have sustained the aggregate campaign contribution limits approved in *Buckley*.

Buckley and *McCutcheon* elevated the right of free speech under the First Amendment over Congress's power under Article I to prevent campaign contributions and expenditures from corrupting the election process. It did so where the plaintiff, McCutcheon, had donated funds to 16 different candidates, which in the aggregate totaled $33,088. He claimed that the aggregate campaign

134 DAVID L. NELSON

contribution limits of FECA and BCRA prevented him from making contributions to 12 additional candidates or their committees, thereby depriving him of freedom of speech. Nothing stopped him under *Buckley* from making as many separate independent expenditures favoring other candidates as he chose.

Not only did the Court's three decisions—*Buckley, McCutcheon* and *Citizens United*—eviscerate two laws adopted by Congress to safeguard elections from corruption and the appearance of corruption, they emasculated Congress's Article I powers and the powers reserved to the states under the Tenth Amendment to place limits on political donations and campaign financing. The Court left Congress and the states no room to legislate future limits on campaign contributions and expenditures other than individual candidate and candidate committee caps, the regulation of transfers between political committees or cases of outright bribery. Data compiled by the Center for Responsive Politics and posted on its site OpenSecrets.org, shows that average contributions to members of the House of Representatives by gun rights groups sharply spiked following the decision in *Citizens United* rising from an average of $4,400 in 2010 to $10,000 in 2016. For U.S. Senators the data shows an even sharper spike in the average contribution from gun rights groups, from about $5,500 in 2010 to $29,000 in 2016.[53] The Appendix speaks for itself. We are left with a government of the dollar, by the dollar, and for the dollar that can only be corrected by a different Supreme Court or a constitutional amendment.

The Court is one of our most revered and noblest institutions. But over the long arc of history, these decisions will be severely questioned and criticized by legal scholars and jurists. Consider that the Supreme Court's decision in *Dred Scot,*[54] which held that a black man born in the United States was not a citizen because his ancestors had been brought here as slaves, has become an egregious example of judicial excess. It took the Thirteenth Amendment following the Civil War to abolish slavery and correct that one. At the same time the Fourteenth Amendment was adopted. Its first sentence reads: "All persons born or naturalized in the United States and subject to the jurisdiction thereof, are citizens of the United States and of the state wherein they reside."

Corporations are not people or natural persons—they cannot be born, nor can they be naturalized, nor do they reside in homes. They cannot choose the nation's representatives because they are not citizens for purposes of our elections. We, the people, created the United States of America when the Continental Congress formally declared the name of the new nation to be the "United States" of America on September 9, 1776.[55] The nation we the people created belongs *to the people who created it*. Recall that England had sought to control the colonies through the use of chartered corporations that repeatedly violated the freedom and safety of the colonists. The Revolutionary War corrected that problem.

In short, the Supreme Court's decisions in *Heller, McDonald, Buckley, Citizens United,* and *McCutcheon* have stifled Congressional and state powers to legislate gun control. In those five opinions the Court struck the words *well-regulated militia* from the Second Amendment, announced a private right to bear arms, made that right binding on the states through one or the other clauses of the Fourteenth Amendment, and told us that the First Amendment right of free speech permits an unlimited flow of money from wealthy citizens and corporate treasuries into our political elections. As a result of those Supreme Court decisions, we now live in a fast growing gun culture and political campaign contribution environment where the lives of our public officials and the safety of every man, woman, and child in America are at risk. We are no longer safe in our homes, on our streets, in public places, or even in the sanctity of our houses of worship. Our basic freedoms and the constitutional underpinnings of our republic are now at grave risk. The many acts described in this book proclaim that the time to enact common sense explosives and firearms regulation is now. We can no longer wait.

There is hope. The Stoneman Douglas high school students and their followers may be facing a Goliath sustained by First, Second, and Fourteenth Amendment claims, campaign finance laws, and court decisions, but take heart. They are getting their message out. On April 12, 2018, the *Detroit Free Press* reported that Bank of America would stop lending to business clients that manufactured military-style weapons for civilian use.[56] In response to recent mass shooting incidents, Costco has banned customers from carrying guns into their stores. Many major retailers (Walmart, Kroger, and CVS, for example) are requesting that customers not openly carry guns into their stores.[57] To confront gun violence challenges confronting its broader business, American Outdoors Brands announced it was spinning off its Smith and Wesson firearms unit on November 15, 2019. It said the decision was reached as a result of, ". . . significant changes in the political climate, as well as the economic, investing, and insurance markets."[58]

Recently internal struggles within the NRA have been in the news. Litigation between the NRA and Ackerman McQueen, an advertising firm that worked for the NRA for decades, was filed. The NRA claimed that Ackerman McQueen had smeared its reputation; Ackerman McQueen countersued claiming the NRA had smeared its reputation.[59] Oliver North was ousted as the NRA's chief executive following North's alleged attempt to oust Wayne LaPierre at the NRA annual convention in April, 2019. Then the NRA suspended Christopher W. Cox, its second in command, contending that he had participated in the alleged coup against LaPierre. Cox responded that the claims against him were unfair and patently false.[60] It has also been reported that wealthy NRA supporters are seeking the ouster of LaPierre.[61] In July of 2019 it was reported that the attorney general for the District of Columbia had opened an investigation against the NRA to examine how funds moved between the NRA and its charity the NRA Foundation. That investigation also seeks to determine if money was properly used for charitable purposes.[62]

The NRA currently has fewer allies in Congress than it had ten years ago. It has been reported that in 2008 there were 57 Democrats in the House of Representatives to whom the NRA had assigned an A rating, and 157 to whom it had assigned an F rating. The NRA gives an A rating "to signify consistent support for gun rights and opposition to restrictions on gun rights," and assigns an F rating to those who do not. After the 2018 midterm election cycle there were 3 Democrats in the House of Representatives with an A rating and 243 with an F rating.[63] Later, Letitia James, the New York Attorney General, listed Josh Powell, former Chief of Staff, and Wayne LaPierre, in a lawsuit that alleged the fraudulent use of charitable funds, and asked that the NRA be dissolved. Mr. Powell has himself written a book (Inside the NRA A Tell All Account of Corruption, Greed, and Paranoia Within the Most Powerful Political Group in America, Grand Central Publishing 9/8/2020) in which he criticizes the NRA's use of charitable funds.

In April of 2013, following the massacre at the Sandy Hook elementary school in Newtown, Connecticut, the United States Senate voted down bills to expand background checks and to ban assault weapons. Galvanized by the defeat of those bills, parents from Sandy Hook swung into action and began to organize. Several groups have formed to compete with the NRA.

- "Americans for Responsible Action" founded by former U.S. Representative Gabrielle Giffords following the incident in Tucson (see Chapter 6 above).

- "Moms Demand Action" created by Shannon Watts.

- "Sandy Hook Promise" organized by Nicole Hockley and Mark Barden to create programs to train classmates to recognize danger signs.

- "Newtown Action Alliance" organized by Po Murray to support a ban on assault weapons.

- "Moms Demand Action" joined Michael Bloomberg's group "Mayors against Illegal Guns" to form "Everytown for Gun Safety." Mayor Bloomberg is an avid promoter of gun safety.

- After Parkland the students there organized "March for Our Lives."

It has been suggested that the groups who favor common sense gun regulation should join and form a single lobbying body to counter the effect of the NRA. That process has started with Everytown for Gun Safety. During the 2018 midterm elections, in a dramatic break with the past, gun control groups outspent the NRA and gun control candidates began to win elections.[64] The March for our Lives group published a plan in August of 2019 to secure responsible gun control. Some of their proposals appear in Chapter 15 below. So yes, there is hope that change will come, that the will of the majority will prevail.

It's thrilling to see this happen. It reminds one of the ants that moved the rubber tree plant. Now the nation must focus on a defined goal. What should a statute that creates a new national policy on gun ownership and carriage look like? And how can such a statute come to be?

CHAPTER **14**

The Road to Common Sense Gun Control

Our children deserve an honest debate and a serious attempt at comprehensive gun control.
— Michael Paterson, a Fellow of the American Academy of Emergency Medicine - Editorial, Detroit Free Press, April 1, 2018.

The physician quoted above, self-described as an avid hunter, has served in a number of medical facilities. He treated victims of car bombings in Iraq and victims riddled with bullets from military assault weapons at emergency departments including Henry Ford Hospital in Detroit, Michigan.

Dr. Paterson heard the "clarion bell sound six times in one night signaling the arrival of six gunshot victims" and the "tinkle of bullet fragments and jackets hitting the floor" as victims were loaded onto operating tables. His profession immersed him in the carnage created by lax gun laws. He should be thanked profusely for his column—it should be required reading for all political and judicial candidates for public office.

Ominous signs are appearing in the news media. A *New York Times* editorial on August 17, 2019, reported that there are now 15 million military assault-style rifles in civilian hands in the United States and that it is now too late to ban them. The editorial concedes that military assault weapons are rarely used in suicides or crimes but that, "... when they are (used) the bloodshed is appalling."[1]

Gun deaths within the United States now greatly exceed those of any other industrialized nation in the world. The statistics portend a bleak future. The Gun Violence Archive reported that during 2019 the United States suffered 254 mass shootings as of August 9, 2019. It defined a mass shooting as an incident where four people other than the shooter were killed or injured. The Gun Violence Archive tallied 8,972 gun deaths from January 1 up to August of 2019.

It was startling to read on August 7, 2019, following the mass shooting in El Paso, Texas, that Amnesty International had issued a warning to travelers coming to America from abroad that they should exercise extreme caution due to *rampant gun violence* that is so prevalent it amounts to *a human rights crisis.*[2] Other countries have also advised their citizens not to travel to the United States due to high levels of gun violence.[3] When did we lose sight of the devastating injuries that military assault weapons inflict? How long does it take for mass murder to fade from the news cycle?

We do not have tape recordings or video clips of what the delegates said in Philadelphia in Convention Hall or what the members of that first Congress said later in New York when they created the Bill of Rights. But we can be pretty certain what they would say after reading Dr. Paterson's guest column, *The New York Times* editorial, or the warning from Amnesty International. In *Heller,* the Supreme Court pushed the words "well regulated militia" aside in order to articulate a limited private right to bear arms. That left us with the same problem our first Congress tried to sort through in New York. What did James Madison, who drafted the Second Amendment, and more importantly the members of our first Congress, mean when they placed the words, "a well regulated militia", in the Second Amendment? How does what they ratified over 220 years ago relate to today? Unfortunately, the Founding Fathers are not here to help us.

Establishing the rule of law to preserve domestic tranquility was a fundamental consideration when our Founding Fathers created the United States government. Our Constitution elegantly stated in its preamble that it was ordained by the people of the United States to, among other things ". . . establish justice, *insure domestic tranquility,* provide for the common defense, promote the general welfare and secure the blessings of liberty, to ourselves and our posterity." Currently, our gun laws are destroying domestic tranquility.

At Gettysburg in the midst of a Civil War, President Lincoln stated our new nation was conceived in liberty. In honor of the fallen soldiers, he asked that we take "increased devotion to the task for which they gave the last full measure of devotion" and "highly resolve that these dead shall not have died in vain—that this nation, under God, shall have a new birth of freedom—and that government of the people, by the people, for the people, shall not perish from the earth."[4] He told us in a few classic words that America's experiment with democracy and the vitality of the freedoms it created depended on its people.

The government Lincoln spoke of will not be preserved, and it will perish if our leaders do not honor their oath of office. Our elected representatives have an obligation to listen to their constituents, certainly, but when they genuflect before special interest groups or wealthy contributors, they attack the basic principles of our republic and put it at grave risk. That threat will only be met in regard to gun violence when the American people acting through their elected representatives restore balance to the right to bear arms.

So far, America's history with the right to bear arms, innovative gun designs, and campaign finance regulation have produced an ill-defined private right to bear arms, military assault weapons like the AK 47, the AR-15, and parts to accelerate their firing rate, online instructions for print-your-own plastic guns, mass shootings, school shootings, accessible firearms for domestic abusers and suicide victims, unlimited corporate campaign contributions, and a Congress that refuses to act.

What next? Background checks alone cannot solve our overwhelming gun problem. Nor will a Johnny-come-lately semiautomatic ban alone get the job done. The problem created by the multitude of guns and parts for them now being manufactured, the multitude already privately owned, and the easy transportation and transfer of guns in a population of 327 million people won't go away with quick fixes. Nor will *Heller* be reversed any time soon. Proposals being put forth to change our gun laws and to bring gun violence under control include the following.

A. Repeal the Second Amendment or Replace It with Clearer Language

The late Supreme Court Justice John Paul Stevens recently wrote in a guest editorial published in *The New York Times* that:

Concern that a national standing army might pose a threat to the security of the separate states led to the adoption of that amendment, which provides that "a well regulated [sic] militia, being necessary to the security of a free state, the right of the people to keep and bear arms, shall not be infringed." Today that concern is a relic of the eighteenth century.... Overturning that decision via a constitutional amendment to get rid of the Second Amendment would be simple and would do more to weaken the NRA's ability to stymie legislative debate and block constructive gun control legislation than any other available option.[5]

Earlier in his book *Six Amendments How and Why We Should Change The Constitution*, Little Brown and Company, First Edition, April 2014, Justice Stevens had suggested that the Second Amendment be amended to read: "A well regulated Militia, being necessary to the security of a free State, the right of the people to keep and bear Arms when serving in the Militia shall not be infringed."

Justice Stevens's proposals have considerable weight, considering their source, but would undoubtedly face tough sledding in a Congress that cannot adopt a statute to place terrorists on the no-fly list into the FBI's Brady background check system.

The Court's lengthy opinion in *Heller* reveals that the Second Amendment is at best ambiguous. One draft that James Madison wrote suggested this wording: "The right of the people to keep and bear arms shall not be infringed; a well-armed and well-regulated militia being the best security of a free country: but no person religiously scrupulous of bearing arms shall be compelled to render military service in person."[sic][6]

Madison's draft reversed the order of the two clauses from that ratified in the Second Amendment, and perhaps more strongly implies that the right to bear arms relates to military uses only. Some of the Founding Fathers feared that the establishment of a powerful national standing army would threaten state militia units. Slave-owning states would not tolerate the loss of their militias. State militias were critical in colonial days given the fact that the settlers had no standing army or state police forces to protect them. It would have been natural for James Madison to assume that the right to bear arms he wrote into the Second Amendment referred only to militia purposes. Self-defense, hunting, and recreational uses were not even mentioned. Military assault weapons like those being sold today came on the scene much later. But given today's gun culture and political realities Madison's draft language would probably have fared no better in today's Supreme Court than the language used in the Second Amendment.

It might be more palatable to some if a proposal to amend the Second Amendment was offered that read:

> The right to bear firearms specifically suited for self-defense, hunting, and recreational uses shall not be infringed. Military assault weapons and explosive devices shall not be owned or carried except by duly constituted and well-regulated members of the United States military, police, and militia forces or state and municipal military, police, and militia forces. Congress shall have power to define, limit, and regulate the use of all firearms and explosive devices consistent with this Amendment.

But it is highly unlikely that Congress will repeal the Second Amendment or enact a replacement. Either would have to run the gauntlet of vigorous challenges in the states. It would require years of patient, determined effort to get the states to adopt it. Even if all of that happened, Congress would *still* have the task of fleshing it out with a uniform national law.

B. Ask the Supreme Court in New Cases to Clarify its Rulings in *Heller* and *MacDonald*, Balance the Rights of Gun Owners and Those Seeking Gun Regulation, and Clarify the Power of Congress and our State Legislatures to Enact New Laws.

Heller invited new legislation. That is confirmed by some concluding statements in Justice Scalia's opinion:

> And there will be time enough to expound upon the historical justifications for the exceptions we have mentioned if and when those exceptions come before us.... But the enshrinement of Constitutional rights necessarily takes certain policy choices off the table. These include the absolute prohibition of handguns held and used in the home for self-defense.[7]

An "if and when" approach is problematic. The Supreme Court cannot act unless Congress or the states act first. Currently the U.S. Senate refuses to even consider new laws. Congress and state legislatures have been neutralized by the gun lobby and political threats. Without new laws no new cases will arise that would provide the Court with an opportunity to flesh out the right to bear arms as *Heller* suggests.

We hear *balance of power,* but more often than not our elected representatives don't drill down to the concept embedded in those words. Justice is portrayed not only as blind but also as a lady holding balanced scales. Balance is essential if freedom, justice, and domestic tranquility are to prevail. The Founding Fathers designed the American Constitution to balance governmental power between federal and state powers and among legislative, executive, and judicial powers. A system of laws that relies on a balance of power is like a mobile hung from the ceiling; it resembles the balance that exists in our solar system. It takes a whole lot of energy within the mobile and our solar system to harness and balance the forces trying to pull them apart. True, the Court's opinion in *Heller* announced a private right to bear arms, but as revealed in the quotation from Justice Scalia above it is also a primer on how that right is limited. *Heller* is an invitation to balance the rights of gun owners to own and carry against those who seek gun safety regulations. The nation must accept that invitation and act on it if gun violence is to be brought under control.

The preamble of the Constitution proclaims that the United States government is derived from the people. However, a nation of 327 million people cannot all write the laws that govern them. Public opinion plays a large role in establishing public policy to be sure, but we depend on the good sense and judgment of our elected representatives to write our laws, our presidents to execute them, and our judges to interpret and enforce them. As Benjamin Franklin said, we are a republic.

Article VI provides that the Constitution and laws duly made under the authority of the United States are to be the supreme law of the land. That tersely states our fundamental and guiding principle—the rule of law. It may be fashionable to believe the Supreme Court creates our laws, but that is not what the Constitution provides. Article I unambiguously states that *all* legislative powers of the United States government are vested in Congress.

Even though the Constitution grants veto power to the President, Congress can override a presidential veto. The Constitution does not provide for enacting laws by referendum, executive fiat, or judicial pronouncement. Division of power created the pillars of our Constitution.

In Article III the judicial power of the United States was vested in "one supreme Court [sic], and in such inferior courts as the Congress may from time to time ordain and establish."[8] The Supreme Court has no power to introduce or enact new laws, and it is wrongheaded to interpret *Marbury v. Madison* or Chief Justices Marshall or Hughes to have said that. The Supreme Court interprets the Constitution and laws enacted by Congress, state legislatures, or municipal governments in cases brought before the Court, but it must follow those laws if they do not violate the Constitution. Chief Justice Marshall told us we are a nation of laws. The gun rights proponents' stance that the answer to gun violence is a good guy with a gun must be discarded. It is a frontal attack on the principle that Chief Justice Marshall so profoundly stated.

It does not belabor the obvious to say these things. The words that created our government, quoted above, are not trite expressions for politicians to trot out on the campaign trail or at Fourth of July celebrations. You cannot understand the meaning of particular clauses of the Constitution by plucking them out one at a time. You must consider the whole document to discern the intent of the Founders. It is part of the glue that holds the American experiment in government by the people together.

Another Second Amendment case is presently before the Supreme Court. New York City recently enacted an ordinance regulating the transportation of guns within the city. Residents with so-called premise licenses were authorized to transport their weapons to seven shooting ranges within the city limits, but the ordinance banned the transportation of guns anywhere else including second homes and shooting ranges outside of the city. The ordinance was challenged by The New York State Rifle and Pistol Association and three city residents in the Federal District Court in Manhattan and that court's decision upholding the ordinance was appealed to the United States Court of Appeals for the Second Circuit. A panel of the three judges on the latter court unanimously upheld the District Court's opinion. "Then, anticipating an appeal to the United States Supreme Court, New York rescinded the ordinance." On April 27, 2020, the Supreme Court dismissed the appeal on grounds it was moot. The case is seen as critical to Second Amendment rights because, although lower courts have issued something like 1000 rulings concerning *Heller* and *MacDonald*, the Supreme Court has not considered a Second Amendment case for a decade.[9]

C. Appoint a Presidential Commission to Study Gun Violence and Recommend New Gun Laws

To establish a definitive, common sense national policy on gun control, the President could appoint a national commission of experts and legal scholars similar to the Warren Commission. If Congress funded it and provided it with subpoena power it might work. Some of the many issues such a Commission could investigate and report on include:

- Should the Second Amendment be repealed or replaced with new language?

- What limits should be placed on the right to bear arms declared in *Heller*?

- What weapons are "highly dangerous firearms," as referred to in *Heller*, that may be banned or more intensely regulated?

- Can the Brady Background Check system be expanded to all points of sale or transfer including gun shows, internet sales, and sales by end users?

- Who are the "law-abiding, responsible citizens" Justice Scalia referred to in *Heller* who are entitled to exercise a Second Amendment right to bear civilian firearms?

- Should red flag laws that ban firearms from the possession of domestic abusers or potential suicide victims be enacted or expanded?

- Should laws that define the manner in which civilian firearms may be carried in public places (e.g., openly, concealed, disabled, encased, or locked) be enacted?

- Should laws be enacted to define "sensitive places" such as schools and government buildings" where civilian firearms are banned?

- Should a federal excise or sales tax be imposed on all sales and transfers of civilian firearms and on parts, accessories and ammunition for them to help fund regulation?

- Should immunity statutes that protect manufacturers, dealers, and end users from legal liability resulting from violations of gun laws or negligence be repealed?

- Should dealers and end users be required to carry personal injury and property damage liability insurance to protect the public?

Powerful interest groups lobby against gun control laws, our politicians rely on campaign contributions from the lobbyists and kowtow to them, and too many voters support them or look the other way. That is not what the rule of law is about; it puts us on the road to oligarchy.* Perhaps a Presidential Commission to recommend new laws would clear away some of the fog and point the way forward, but given the current political stalemate it is doubtful that one could be appointed or funded or that any of its proposals would ever be adopted by Congress. Under our constitution the onus is on Congress to investigate new gun laws and enact them into being.

D. Target Key Areas of Control through Piecemeal Federal Legislation

Key areas of concern at the federal level include a renewal of the assault rifle and extended magazines ban, a ban of bump stocks, expansion of the Brady Act National Instant Criminal Background Check System to all points of sale, and adoption of red flag laws. These proposals have considerable merit, but do not deal with the reality of over 350 million firearms already held in a population of 327 million. That arsenal includes AK-47s, AR-15s, extended loading devices, high velocity ammunition and kits for guns you can build yourself.[10] It continues to grow and is now the elephant in the room.

The current stalemate over gun control came into sharp focus after the 2018 midterm elections when Democrats assumed

_____
*A small group of people having control of a country, organization, or institution. Government by such a group.

control of the U.S. House of Representatives—but not of the Senate. On February 28, 2019, the House voted 240 to 190 to require background checks on all gun purchasers including those seeking to buy guns at gun shows and over the internet.[11] The following day the House voted 228 to 198 to strengthen Brady background checks by increasing the number of days a seller must wait for a response to a request for a background check before completing a gun sale from three to at least ten days.[12] Both bills were rational responses to the March for Life protest that followed the 2018 massacres at Mandalay Bay, Sutherland, Texas, and Parkland, Florida. Public opinion polls indicated wide support for both measures. President Trump at first stated that if the Senate did vote to approve he would veto both bills. A two-thirds vote by the House and the Senate is needed to override a presidential veto. Even after the terrorist attack in El Paso in July 2019, the Majority Leader of the Senate refused to bring either House bill before the Senate for a hearing or a vote. After El Paso, President Trump reversed his position and suggested he would accept expanded background checks, but he offered no specific proposals to do so. At this writing the two bills continue to languish in the Senate.

No language has been found in the Constitution that provides a majority leader of a political party power to block legislation from coming to the floor of the Senate for an up or down vote. Congress has tied itself up in knots through arcane rules that give the majority leader power to control legislation and that allow filibusters to the extent it is no longer capable of even considering gun control laws. Article I, Section 5 of the Constitution provides that ". . . Each House shall keep a Journal of its Proceedings . . . and the Yeas and Nays of the Members of either House, on any question shall at the Desire of one fifth of those Present, be entered in the Journal." But Yeas and Nays were never taken on the gun control bills now on the Majority Leaders desk in the Senate. Both measures were tabled without a single vote, journal entry, or even a word of debate.

E. Expand the Brady Background Check System

Expanding the Brady Act background check system needs special mention. It is a valuable tool but not enough. As currently mandated, it does not provide a robust procedure for *licensing* only those fit to own and carry firearms. Over 327 million people live in the United States. They move around and change their names.

Their physical and mental states change—sometimes day to day. Mental health issues may not be recorded or even diagnosed. If records are kept, they may be "siloed" from other databases, or they may be protected from disclosure by confidentiality laws. Databases such as the U.S. government's Terrorist Screening Database (which includes the No-Fly list) are omitted from the Brady Act's National Instant Criminal Background Check System.

Nor do agencies always report required mental health or arrest data to the FBI. For example, the Air Force failed to notify the FBI about Devin Patrick Kelley's record before he massacred the parishioners of Sutherland's First Baptist Church. Court orders against domestic abusers are not readily discovered in background checks, nor are indications that persons in private residences are suicidal.

The burden of proving that an applicant is or is not qualified to be entrusted to own and carry firearms should not rest disproportionately on the government's ability to conduct background checks within five days as it does now. An applicant seeking to buy a firearm ought to be required to *prove* that he or she is a law-abiding citizen capable of responsibly and safely owning and carrying firearms. He or she should demonstrate successful completion of rigorous safety courses, undergo a more thorough Brady background check, and be required to submit military service records. The period for conducting the background check should be expanded. Brady background checks should include a more robust procedure for discovering court protective orders involving firearms or domestic violence. That is the kind of information that licensing laws require in other areas such as medicine or law. It ought to apply to the purchase, possession, and transfer of guns as well.

F. Leave Gun Control to the States

The Fourth Circuit Court of Appeals in Richmond, Virginia, recently upheld a Maryland law that imposed limits by banning the sale of 45 kinds of assault weapons and large capacity magazines. In his majority opinion in *Kolbe v. Hogan*, Judge Robert King wrote, "Put simply, we have no power to extend Second Amendment protection to the weapons of war that the *Heller* decision explicitly excluded from such coverage."[13] The Supreme Court turned down an appeal of that ruling.[14] Massachusetts District Court Judge William Young ruled that assault weapons are military firearms beyond the reach of the constitutional right to bear arms.[15] On July 27, 2018, the Michigan Supreme Court ruled that Michigan's Ann Arbor and Clio school districts had a right to ban guns from their schools.[16]

That's one way to refine the right, but it entails a time-consuming state-by-state enactment of laws that results in lengthy, costly litigation, appeals and reversals on appeal. Historically and by design, state gun laws lack uniformity. Congress has power to impose uniform statutes applicable nationwide, but it hasn't. Instead it has introduced laws to expand the private right to bear firearms. Congressional Republicans recently advanced legislation to enable travelers to carry handguns across state lines by requiring a state forbidding open carry to recognize as valid an open carry permit issued by another state.[17] If that measure becomes a template for future legislation, the weakest state gun laws become the law of the land. Enacting gun control laws at the state level are not a workable solution to the nation's existing gun problem.

G. Pattern New Federal Gun Laws on Those Adopted in Other Nations

Other nations have tougher gun laws than those in the United States. Following the Port Arthur massacre of 1996 in Australia, that nation and all its states and territories adopted the National Firearms Agreement, which banned semiautomatics and some other self-loading rifles and shotguns. They also implemented standard licensing and permit criteria, storage requirements and inspections, and greater restrictions on the sale of firearms and ammunition. Australia's new laws required license applicants to take safety courses and to show a genuine reason for owning a firearm. Australia's new standards imposed a 28-day waiting period for purchasing a gun and provided for denial of a gun permit where there was reliable evidence of a mental or physical condition that rendered an applicant unsuitable. Australia also established a program to buy back prohibited weapons. According to two studies in 2010 the rate of gun homicides in Australia from 1995 to 2006 fell 59 percent.[18]

On Friday, March 15, 2019, a gunman armed with a semiautomatic rifle shot and killed 50 Muslims gathered at two mosques in Christchurch, New Zealand and wounded more than 40 others, many of them critically, in the worst mass murder in New Zealand's history.[19] News reports identified the assailant as Brenton

Harrison Tarrant, but indicated there may have been additional gunmen. Before the attack Tarrant reportedly posted an anti-Muslim manifesto on the internet. During the attack he wore a camera strapped to his forehead to stream video of the massacre on Facebook Live to ensure worldwide dispersal on the internet. Within two days of the massacre, New Zealand's Prime Minister, Jacinda Ardern, vowed that New Zealand's gun laws would change,[20] and New Zealanders began to turn in their semiautomatics.[21]

New Zealand's response to the Christchurch massacre sharply contrasts with the response to similar massacres in the United States where for years people have flocked to purchase guns following a massacre and new gun laws have been thwarted. In response to the carnage inflicted by the El Paso terrorist the United States Senate ignored new bills by the House of Representatives and let them languish. The difference is that within one week New Zealand did something about it and we didn't.

Following a mass shooting in Nova Scotia where 22 people died, Canada adopted an immediate ban on what its prime minister described as, "military style assault weapons."[22] The experience of Australia and New Zealand with their new gun laws should be studied. Gun regulation in Canada, England, Japan, Switzerland, and other nations should also be studied. Why aren't our leaders doing that?

H. Use the Ballot Box to Elect Political Leaders Who Are Committed to Common Sense Gun Control Solutions

Our gun laws, or the absence of them, tell us up front that the gun lobby is writing the script. Like pornography, we know it when we see it.* Despite homicide statistics and investigative reports like those the *Detroit Free Press* and *New York Times* published, gun stores and gun shows in the United States remain festooned with semiautomatic rifles and handguns, bump stocks, extended clips and magazines, and cartons of high-tech ammunition. Visit one. Examine the fire power on display. Read the ads and literature accompanying them. They go far beyond weapons needed to defend one's home or hunt ducks. Ask yourself if what you see there is reasonable. Pick up a copy of magazines like *Firearms News* and read it. Watch YouTube videos of shooters getting their

---

*Phrase made famous by Justice Potter Stewart to describe his threshold test for determining obscenity in *Jacobellis v. Ohio*. (And in his view, the film *The Lovers* was not obscene.)

kicks bump-firing their semiautomatics. Afterward, ask yourself again if any of what you've seen strikes you as reasonable?

We already have 15 million military assault-style rifles in our midst. If existing gun laws stay in place how many *more* millions will spread throughout the population? Will future citizens walk around with advanced AK-47s and stand their ground? And should that happen, how can the mayhem be stopped? Silence and inaction have deadly consequences for all of us and create an existential threat to our nation.

It is not enough to wring our hands and lament—as some do—that the shooter spraying bullets into the theater audience in Aurora was unbalanced. That the shooters with semiautomatic rifles in Las Vegas and Stoneman Douglas were unstable, or that the El Paso shooter was a domestic terrorist. It is not enough to offer heartfelt prayers or to build memorials outside a blood-soaked killing ground. If there are mass murderers and terrorists among us, why do we permit military-style firearms and bandoliers of ammunition to move though commerce and end up in their hands?

When all the options are considered, it is clear that the nation will never decide which gun control policy decisions may not be taken off the table nor will it enshrine any of the limitations, qualifications, and exceptions to the private right to bear arms envisioned in *Heller* into constitutional law unless Congress exercises its powers and legislates sensible gun control into being. That is how our laws are enacted, executed, interpreted, and enforced. The people rely on the ballot box to select and control our representatives, certainly. But they also rely on the oath of office administered to our leaders as they assume the duties of their office. The Constitution requires that they swear to protect and defend the Constitution.[23]

The passion of the Stoneman Douglas students, of other students and parents lining up behind them nationwide, and of groups seeking rational gun regulation, must be channeled to succeed. Grass roots movements have proven they can succeed. Activists worked from World War II ("Old enough to fight, old enough to vote") to 1971 to ratify the Twenty-sixth Amendment to lower the voting age to 18 years. The Civil Rights movement found legal expression in the Civil Rights Act of 1964. Not perfect, but that law, coming hard on the heels of freedom marches and the assassination of President Kennedy, who had sought its enactment, laid down a marker. Working together using that passion, a new generation of lawmakers not tied to the existing political structure must enact new laws that answer the questions posed earlier, fill in the blanks left by *Heller* and *McDonald,* and regulate the right to bear arms. If the current Congress and President shy away from enacting common sense gun laws, then let's elect leaders who will.

I. Enact a Federal Comprehensive Uniform Gun Control Statute that Is Drawn from the Limitations and Exceptions to the Second Amendment Described in *Heller* and from a Plan Proposed by the Stoneman Douglas Students

Those seeking sensible gun regulations should not despair. The path forward may be loaded with landmines, including campaign finance hurdles created by *Citizen's United*, but the movement initiated by the Stoneman Douglas students is picking up steam. It promises to break the gun law impasse in Washington, D.C., if it stays focused on the constitutional foundations of the United States government. On August 22, 2019, *The New York Times* reported that the Stoneman Douglas survivors had produced a plan to control guns. Their plan included a national licensing and registration system (with multiple steps of licensing including ten-day waiting periods and mandatory license renewal periods), a ban on assault weapons and high capacity magazines, a mandatory gun buyback program for assault weapons, limits on firearm purchases, a national director of gun violence prevention, raising the minimum age of gun purchasers to 21, and a Peace Corps-style program to recruit young people to promote gun violence prevention.[24]

The Stoneman Douglas plan provides a window of opportunity. Additional evidence that the climate for gun control is improving came when the former mayor of New York City, Michael Bloomberg, also embraced national gun licensing, stricter background checks, red flag laws, and a revival of the assault weapon ban during his campaign to become the nominee of the Democrat Party for 2020 Presidential election [25]

Even though *Heller* and *McDonald* concerned legislation that went too far by completely banning firearms in the home, common sense dictates that a generalized law-abiding citizen concept will not identify those who by age, temperament, training, and experience can upon application be *safely licensed* to possess and use firearms. And a generalized concept like *Heller's* weapons in common use at the time is hopelessly insufficient. Firearms are easily transported across state lines. Fragmented state laws or piecemeal Congressional enactments cannot supply uniform definitions, limitations on the right to carry firearms, or enforcement.

On one side of the debate, a mass of the electorate demands the right to bear arms for self-defense, hunting, and recreation. The right of self-defense protected in *Heller* is a natural right that should be preserved. To be sure these uses of firearms present hazards, but the right to bear firearms made for those purposes poses no unreasonable risk to public safety. But open carry in public places, mass murder, use of guns *inside* the home to commit domestic violence, and semiautomatic assault weapons *do*.

Some argue that the wide dispersal of guns among the populace diminishes crime and violence because perpetrators are deterred by fear of retaliation. That theory collapses when it is realized that more guns in the hands of private citizens is the catalyst that produces an ever increasing need for weapons of self-defense. It collapses in the face of ballooning crime statistics and escalating mass murder. It completely collapses when you compare the American experience to that of other nations like Australia and New Zealand.

In the macho world of gun enthusiasts, it is not politically correct to advocate the regulation of firearms. When the subject comes up after each horrific tragedy, politicians run for cover. Many shrug their shoulders and say: *Forget it; new laws and regulations will be as easily evaded as those now on the books.* That excuse can be said of any law.

On the other side of the debate, proponents of gun control assert private citizens don't need military assault weapons; they have no place in civilized society. They want limits placed on firearms to protect society. They want firearms kept away from persons unfit to bear them. They want safe schools, streets, and public venues, and effective universal background checks.

Sound arguments can be made for the positions of both sides, but these two groups must find common ground. Separating firearms suited for civilian uses from those designed for military use fits the language of the Second Amendment and the holding in

Heller and offers a rational point of departure. The Court stated that an absolute ban by the federal government (*Heller*) or by a state instrumentality (*McDonald*) on the ownership and use of a functional, loaded handgun in the home for self-defense is unconstitutional. But the Court in *Heller* did not find a *constitutional* right to own and carry a firearm in any other place or for any other purpose. It described the right as a "not unlimited right." When he wrote the majority opinion in *Heller*, Justice Scalia had to come to grips with the same gun safety problem that James Madison and the delegates faced at that first Congress when they drew up the Second Amendment. Madison used the words *well-regulated.* Justice Scalia chose *a not unlimited right.*

Justice Scalia also acknowledged the historical tradition of prohibiting the carrying of dangerous and unusual weapons.[26] Recall again that *Heller* and *McDonald* concerned laws that banned handguns in the home. Claims by gun rights proponents that an AR-15 is not a military assault weapon, for example, miss the point. Under the reasoning of *Heller,* it may be banned from civilian use if found, in the words of Justice Scalia, to be a dangerous and unusual weapon. Limitations that Justice Scalia described (discussed in Chapter 3 above) pertaining to the carriage of machine guns and semiautomatic firearms; the carriage of concealed firearms; the carriage of firearms by convicted felons and the mentally ill; and restrictions on guns in streets and public buildings point the way forward. Congress should study *Heller*'s limitations, qualifications, and exceptions, and enact them into law.

The Gifford's Law Center To Prevent Gun Violence published a "Post - Heller Litigations Summary" in April of 2017that is available on the Internet. The summary tracked 1,150 federal and state post-Heller Second Amendment decisions. The summary concluded that, "Courts have rejected Second Amendment challenges 94% of the time."

The study shows that courts have recognized the validity of Heller's qualifications and limitations on the Second Amendment right to bear arms in the great majority of cases brought to challenge new gun laws.

Article I, Section 8 of the Constitution grants Congress powers to enact laws that regulate the manufacture, sale, ownership, and use of dangerous products such as drugs, motor vehicles, and financial securities. Firearms serve no legitimate purpose other than self-defense, hunting, or use by the military or police, and they are far deadlier by design. Existing federal statutes regulate the sale and transfer of firearms,[27] but not effectively of *all* firearms and ammunition. They are loaded with exceptions and sunset provisions. They don't provide and enforce effective procedures for licensing and regulating manufacturers, transporters, and sellers.

This book shows where to find power to enact new law in the *Heller* and *McDonald* decisions, in the Constitution's interstate Commerce Clause, in its militia powers, in Congress's power to tax, and in its power to pass laws necessary and proper for carrying out its enumerated powers. The recent warning from Amnesty International to potential United States visitors demonstrates that gun violence in the United States is materially obstructing and impacting foreign and domestic commerce. Consider also the growing cost of gun violence.

Aimee Picchi (CBS Moneywatch) recently wrote, ". . . gun violence in the U.S. also has enormous financial cost, rippling through the economy in the form of lost wages, medical bills, higher taxes for law enforcement, and lower property values, among other factors. Some estimates put the total annual tab of shootings at well over $100 billion, while others put it even higher." Picchi reported that Mike McLively, senior staff attorney at Giffords Law Center to Prevent Gun Violence, reported that researchers conservatively estimated the cost of gun violence is at least $229 billion per year.[28] The latter estimate was based on data from the Giffords Law Center to Prevent Gun Violence and the Center for Disease Control and a report published by Carolyn B. Maloney (D.NY), Joint Economic Committee Vice Chair, on September 18, 2019, that estimated gun violence costs in the U. S. in the form of lost wages, medical bills, higher taxes for law enforcement and lower property values, among other factors to be $229 billion a year. That report stated, "The human costs are beyond our ability to comprehend. It is tragic. It is sickening and it is a crisis."

New legislation will meet fierce opposition, but Congress has sufficient power to enact a uniform national law that binds all the states. The rule of law requires that tools come out of the legal toolbox. Licensing laws are such a tool. They regulate lawyers, doctors, motor vehicles, motor vehicle drivers, and, yes, gun owners. Statements in *Heller* that approve licensing laws are critical to finding a way forward. Licensing laws are an excellent regulatory tool that could be employed to identify law-abiding citizens. It is up to Congress to grow a backbone and enact statutes that flesh out the limits, qualifications, and exceptions to the right to bear arms that the Court outlined in *Heller.* Licensing laws are clearly one of those exceptions.

Civil litigation, including the right to jury trial, provides compensation to victims of negligent conduct. It would tell manufacturers, dealers, and other sellers that they have skin in the game. It would also help to keep irresponsible gun owners in line. Criminal laws punish willful violations of statutory requirements and prohibitions. Civil administrative procedures manage claims that regulatory standards have been violated. Mandatory liability and property damage insurance compensates those injured by violations of law or negligence in other areas.

A new national firearms statute can be patterned on the experience gained from testing and licensing motor vehicle drivers, registering motor vehicles and plating them, requiring liability and property damage insurance for motor vehicles, and the adoption of uniform safety standards for motor vehicles as well as the highways on which they are operated. Tools like these can restore a large measure of order to the chaos of gun violence. They put flesh and sinew on the rule of law. They should not be left lying idle in the toolbox.

The use of firearms and explosives to commit homicide, suicide, domestic violence, mass murder, school shootings, and acts of terrorism can only be brought under control through the establishment of a sound regulatory structure that is drawn from the qualifications and exceptions to the Second Amendment right stated in *Heller* and grounded in common sense and the rule of law. The nation now needs to make policy choices that were not considered at that first Congress where protecting state militias was a key concern. With meaningful legislation stalled, we face a burgeoning crisis in our homes, streets, schools, and public places.

Recent events, some bordering on anarchy, make uniform regulation at the federal level imperative. Gun rights activists have become more militant in their opposition to gun control measures, carrying their arms to rallies against gun laws and declaring Second Amendment Sanctuaries. In 2018, Democrats who favored stronger gun laws in the state of Virginia took over the State Legislature. In early January 2020, the Virginia Senate approved several gun control measures including provisions to ban guns in parks and public buildings, to limit hand gun purchases to one each month, to require gun buyers to submit to background checks, and red flag provisions. When the Virginia House of Delegates said it would approve the measures and Virginia's Governor, Ralph Northam, stated he would sign them into law, gun rights activists from all over Virginia and some from as far away as Indianapolis, Indiana, and Fredericksburg, Texas, descended on Richmond to rally against the measures. Many brought their weapons with them including, according to reports, ". . . military-style rifles, shotguns, 9-millimeter handguns, .45- and .22-caliber pistols, and even a .50-caliber sniper rifle." Reports stated that Dick Heller, the lead plaintiff in the *Heller* case, asked the crowd of gun rights supporters, "Do we need gun control in Virginia?" The crowd reportedly responded, "Noooooo."[29] As stated in Chapter 5, the Virginia governor signed a new gun control law on the weekend of April 11, 2020.

On September 1, 2020, during a recent Black Lives Matter protest march a man who claimed he was acting as a private militiaman fired a semiautomatic weapon at protest marchers in Kenosha, Wisconsin killing two persons and wounding another. On September 3, 2020 police officers in Washington state killed a suspect in the shooting death of a right wing activist in Portland, Oregon the previous week.

An incident similar to the one in Virginia occurred in Michigan. During that state's coronavirus emergency declaration, a group of protestors appeared at Michigan's statehouse in Lansing, Michigan, on April 30, 2020, carrying signs protesting the Governor's emergency declaration and crowded out onto the House floor, which is supposed to be off-limits to the general public. It was reported that some of the protestors carried firearms into the visitor's gallery and that one protestor positioned out in front on the Capitol steps carried what he said was a loaded AR-15 rifle.[30]

According to an Associated Press report, by early 2020 more than 100 municipalities in Virginia had designated themselves "sanctuaries" for the Second Amendment that would refuse to recognize state or municipal gun control laws. Referring to the Associated Press report, the *Detroit Free Press* reported on

January 16, 2020, that in Michigan five counties (Macomb, St. Clair, Monroe, Delta, and Marquette) were considering proposals to become Second Amendment sanctuaries. The Free Press article stated the resolutions vary but most declared, ". . . the intention of local officials to oppose 'unconstitutional restrictions' on the Second Amendment right to bear arms."[31]

Chapter 15 sets forth specific suggestions for a new uniform national law to control the current epidemic of gun violence deaths and injuries within the United States and to establish common sense gun regulation. To some the ideas set forth in Chapter 15 may seem Pollyannaish, to others draconian. But lax laws and the formidable gun lobby have created a national crisis where tough regulation is called for. They are in no position to complain. Be that as it may, the proposals and ideas in Chapter 15 are set forth here to those seeking a way forward.

A Proposal for Balanced New Gun Control Laws

E nacting laws and programs like ones the Stoneman Douglas survivors have recommended will not be easy by any means. But if they stick with it and build a platform for enactment in the halls of Congress where honest debate takes place, those who died at Stoneman Douglas, and the thousands killed and maimed in senseless gun violence across our nation, will come to that debate with their loved ones. The Founding Fathers will come with them.

❖

The following proposals do not arise from the author alone. The Stoneman Douglas students suggested many of them in letters to the editor of *The New York Times* following that massacre, and in a plan prepared by March for Our Lives. Chapter 15 expresses the author's view certainly, but also attempts to consolidate proposals gleaned from the many sources listed in this treatise and in the Further Reading section that follows the Appendix.

> *A uniform national law.* A new federal statute—to be called the National Uniform Firearms and Explosives Control Act— should be enacted that incorporates existing federal firearms and explosives laws, amends them, and provides that all state laws that conflict with the new uniform national firearms statute are preempted.

> *A federal firearms control commission.* The agency responsible for administering the new firearms and explosives statute

should be separated from the Bureau of Alcohol, Tobacco, Firearms and Explosives (ATF), given the name Federal Firearms and Explosives Control Commission (FFCC), and given power to administer and enforce the new law. Tobacco and alcohol are consumables. Weapons should be regulated by an agency solely focused on firearms and explosives.

Self-defense. The right to bear arms for self-defense as described in *Heller* should be preserved, subject to regulation as to type of firearm, background checks, licensing and registration, place of carriage, and insurance limitations.

Hunting and recreational uses. Millions of Americans enjoy the right to use firearms for hunting and recreation. The right to possess and carry firearms suited to these purposes should also be preserved subject to regulation as to type of firearm, background checks, licensing and registration, place of carriage, civil liability, and insurance limitations.

Militia uses. A citizen's duty to bear arms as part of a well-regulated militia as stated in Article I and the Second Amendment and referred to in *Heller,* should be brought to bear on the problem of controlling military assault weapons that are now privately held. In modern times, the National Guard, other agencies and police forces, have supplanted the militia, but Congress's power still exists, and it should use that power to call forth and regulate the National Guard as a means of regulating military assault weapons now owned or hereafter acquired by civilians. Units of the National Guard could be made available to protect sensitive areas like schools. The use of firearms for private, unregulated militia purposes (ex: vigilantism) should be banned.

Civilian firearms. The new uniform law should separate military-style weapons from civilian weapons and stringently define the type and number of civilian firearms and the ammunition for them that citizens may possess for permitted civilian uses. Civilian weapons should be described as Category 1 weapons to distinguish them from military-style weapons. The new law should provide for the revision of the weapons classified for civilian purposes as firearms technology develops.

Military-style firearms. The new law should clearly define which weapons are military-style firearms or explosive devices and ban them from civilian use. Military-style firearms should be classified as Category 2 weapons. Explosive devices should be classified as Category 3 weapons. It should provide for revision of the weapons so classified as technology develops. The current machine gun/semiautomatic trigger-pull test should be replaced with a new test that bans the civilian use of firearms and attachments capable of discharging bullets or other projectiles at a rate per minute beyond a stated standard and that bans ammunition with a velocity and penetration force greater than a stated standard.

FFCC firearms laboratory. An FFCC laboratory should be established and staffed with firearms and explosive experts having the credentials necessary to distinguish Category 1 civilian firearms and ammunition from Categories 2 and 3 military-style firearms, ammunition, and explosives as defined in the new law. To provide guidance, the laboratory should regularly publish updated lists of firearms and explosives placed in each category.

– *FFCC buyback program for Category 2 firearms.* The new law should establish a voluntary federal program funded by the federal government and conducted by the FFCC to buy back Category 2 firearms and accessories (together with parts and ammunition for them) from civilians owning them on the date the new law takes effect.

Federal license to own civilian guns. Create a national license to own and carry Category 1 civilian firearms and ammunition for a specified time period and spell out that persons lawfully licensed have a right to possess and carry FFCC-listed weapons for the limited purposes of self-defense, hunting, and recreation. Applicants applying for such a license should be required to pass tests in gun safety and demonstrate in their application that they are law-abiding responsible citizens. A law-abiding citizen should be defined in the new law as one who through age, training, temperament, and commitment can responsibly use and control firearms. It must also provide for applicant reassessments at renewal similar to motor vehicle license retesting and license revocation for violations of the law.

Special License to own military-style (Category 2) firearms. The new law would require that all persons owning Category 2 firearms on the date the new law takes effect who do not elect to participate in the buyback program, would be required to apply within a specified period for a special federal license to own and carry Category 2 firearms and to state in their application the purposes for which a special license to carry Category 2 firearms is needed. Those not participating in the buyback program and who do not obtain a special Category 2 license within the specified period would be required by the new law to turn them over to the FFCC. Upon their failure to comply with a mandatory turnover order within the time specified in the new law, the FFCC would be authorized by the new law to request a warrant from a federal court of competent jurisdiction to recover all Category 2 firearms listed in the mandatory turnover order.

Resale or destruction of Category 2 weapons. The new law should authorize the FFCC to resell all Category 2 firearms it purchases under the buyback program, or that it otherwise acquires under the new law, to federal and state military units, police forces, or licensed dealers, or to shred, crush, or melt them down.

Registration of firearms. Require that all firearms (both Categories 1 and 2) owned by licensees be registered with the FFCC. Provide for microstamping or otherwise permanently affixing registration tags on registered firearms that bear their registration number and are similar to annual registration tags affixed to license plates to identify motor vehicles.

Category 2 military firearms possessed at time of enactment by federal or state military or police forces. Provide that both Category 1 and Category 2 weapons borne by the military, government law enforcement officers, licensed private guards, or by a well-regulated militia or the National Guard units be registered with the FFCC, but otherwise exempted from compliance with the new law. National Guard units could be deployed to protect schools and sensitive public places and to establish order during national emergencies or natural disasters.

Brady background checks. Retain the Brady background check system as part of the new federal licensing procedure but increase the wait period and expand it to all points of sale. Also include in it databases such as the "No-Fly" list and similar databases as they are implemented. Provide for the prompt correction of errors and changed data. A person seeking to purchase a firearm or ammunition for a firearm from a licensed gun dealer, or receiving a firearm or ammunition for a firearm from an existing owner, would establish their bona fides by presenting a valid federal license. The dealer or previous owner would not conduct background checks. The law would require that sales or transfer documents record the license numbers of both the transferor and the transferee and the registration number of the weapon..

Unauthorized sales and transfers. Ban the sale or transfer of both Category 1 (civilian) and Category 2 (military-style) firearms to any person or entity that does not hold a federal license. Provide that transfer or sale of a firearm, firearm parts, or ammunition without *both* parties holding valid federal licenses constitutes a felony. This would include the transfer or disposal of guns owned by persons no longer qualified to be a rightful owner as a result of a change in their circumstances such as death, mental or physical disability, imprisonment, immigration, or similar circumstance. Establish procedures to nullify the right to sell, transfer, or own, by those unfit to do so, or who become unfit or uninsured and for voiding licenses.

Transparency. Establish transparency of FFCC databases as to location of firearms on a reliable, current Internet registry/database of all licensees as well as those determined unfit to purchase, possess, or use firearms. Provide for the prompt correction of errors and changed data.

Public venues. Define the public places, buildings, and gun-free zones where civilians may not carry any firearms whether they hold a firearms license or not.

Transportation of firearms. Regulate the transportation of firearms on all public thoroughfares, railways, waterways, public transport, and similar channels and instruments of interstate commerce, and set standards for carrying firearms—encased, open, concealed, intact, or disassembled—in interstate commerce.

Firearms manufacturers and importers. Provide for grandfathering or renewing existing licenses if the holders meet the law's requirements and for issuing new licenses to those persons and businesses qualified to manufacture, import, or transport firearms to gun dealers in foreign and interstate commerce under the new law. Require that all manufacturers and importers comply with the provisions of the law.

Dealer licensing. Provide for grandfathering or renewing licenses to dealers now holding a license if they meet the law's requirements, provide for issuing new licenses to those persons, businesses, gun shows, and internet sellers that demonstrate they can responsibly sell firearms to federally licensed end users. Require that all dealers comply with the law.

Immunity statutes. Repeal statutes granting manufacturers, dealers, and others immunity from civil suits filed by those injured from the unlawful sale, transfer, possession, carriage, or use of firearms in violation of the law, and provide civil remedies for violations.

Liability and property damage insurance for manufacturers, dealers, and end users. Before any license can issue or renew, require that all persons and entities authorized to receive a license to manufacture, import, sell, transfer, possess, or carry either a Category 1 (civilian) or a Category 2 (military-style) firearm furnish evidence that they maintain public liability insurance with sufficient coverage to reasonably protect the public from a violation of their duties under the new law. The loss of that insurance would result in the suspension of the applicant's license until the insurance was replaced.

A national firearms tax. Levy a national firearms tax on each sale of a firearm, part, or accessory, and on firearm ammunition to help defray the cost of regulation. Sales by the FFCC under the new law, and sales by federal and state military or police units would be exempt from paying the tax.

Fees. Provide a schedule of fees to be paid by manufacturers, dealer license holders, and end-users applying for a federal license or renewal, again to help defray the cost of regulation.

Civil administrative complaints. Provide a procedure for persons in harm's way to protest the ownership and carriage by those not fit. Provide immunity to those who protest and automatic notification of court protective orders or rescissions filed with the registry.

Enforcement of the new law. Establish fines, criminal and civil penalties, provisions for license revocation, and where necessary, confiscation of weapons.

Invoke Congress's commerce, taxation, and militia powers. Employ all of Congress's powers to their fullest extent to carry out the statutory scheme.

APPENDIX

Campaign Expenses Paid by NRA Committees in the 2016 National Elections

The data on the following chart is derived from an FEC report on expenditures paid by the National Rifle Association's Institute for Legislative Action and its Political Victory Fund to support or oppose candidates running in the 2016 national election. It includes information published by Wikipedia on the internet in a document titled, "List of current members of the United States House of Representatives," and a similar document Wikipedia published on the internet titled, "Current members of the United States Senate." To complete the chart, winning and losing candidates were also identified by reference to results of the 2016 election also published on the internet. The political party affiliation of each candidate shown on the chart was obtained from the sources listed above. Asterisks indicate the names of candidates who lost their elections.

The chart does not purport to show any cash contributions made to any candidate listed on the chart by the NRA or its political action committees. It shows only expenditures listed in the FEC report made by the NRA's political action committees named above, to support or oppose candidates running in the 2016 national election. The paid expenses listed in the FEC report include items such as postage and mailing, printing post cards, phone calls, radio, television, and internet advertising, and graphic art design to name but a few. The totals appearing on the chart for each candidate add up all expenses paid for that candidate as listed in the FEC report.

Campaign Expenses Paid by NRA Committees in the 2016 National Elections

Candidate Name	Name						
		Candidate					
Candidate Name	Name	Party	Office	State	Support	Oppose	Total
Angelle, Scott*	NRA of America Political Victory Fund	Rep	HR	LA	$1,725.84		$1,725.84
Ayotte, Kelly A*	NRA Institute for Legislative Action	Rep	SE	NH	$66,322.18		$66,322.18
Babeu, Paul Raymond*	NRA Institute for Legislative Action	Rep	HR	AZ	$13,611.62		$13,611.62
Bacon, Donald	NRA Institute for Legislative Action	Rep	HR	NE	$10,279.45		$10,279.45
Bayh, Evan*	NRA Institute for Legislative Action	Dem	SE	IN		$1,798,984.16	$1,798,984.16
Bayh, Evan*	NRA of America Political Victory Fund	Dem	SE	IN		$648,509.25	$648,509.25
Bennet, Michael	NRA of America Political Victory Fund	Dem	SE	CO		$1,042.88	$1,042.88
Blum, Rodney	NRA Institute for Legislative Action	Rep	HR	IA	$27,589.29		$27,589.29
Blunt, Roy	NRA Institute for Legislative Action	Rep	SE	MO	$240,753.35		$240,753.35
Blunt, Roy	NRA of America Political Victory Fund	Rep	SE	MO	$263,520.00		$263,520.00
Brady, Kevin	NRA of America Political Victory Fund	Rep	HR	TX	$246.40		$246.40
Burr, Richard	NRA Institute for Legislative Action	Rep	SE	NC	$250,470.69		$250,470.69
Burr, Richard	NRA of America Political Victory Fund	Rep	SE	NC	$363,714.73		$363,714.73
Cain, Emily*	NRA Institute for Legislative Action	Dem	HR	ME		$67,763.57	$67,763.57
Cano, Fernando*	NRA of America Political Victory Fund	Dem	HR	NC		$599.56	$599.56
Chabot, Paul R Dr.*	NRA Institute for Legislative Action	Rep	HR	CA	$3,594.38		$3,594.38

Continued ▶

Campaign Expenses Paid by NRA Committees in the 2016 National Elections

Candidate Name	Candidate						
	Name	Party	Office	State	Support	Oppose	Total
Chabot, Steve	NRA Institute for Legislative Action	Rep	HR	CA	$121.85		$121.85
Christensen, Gordon*	NRA of America Political Victory Fund	Dem	HR	MO		$596.44	$596.44
Clinton, Hillary	NRA of America Political Victory Fund	Dem	Pres	US		$7,470,738.05	$7,470,738.05
Clinton, Hillary Rodham	NRA Institute for Legislative Action	Dem	Pres	US		$16,387,239.76	$16,387,239.76
Coffman, Michael	NRA Institute for Legislative Action	Rep	HR	CO	$27,817.45		$27,817.45
Comstock, Barbara J Hon	NRA Institute for Legislative Action	Rep	HR	VA	$58,969.61		$58,969.61
Degner, Kai*	NRA of America Political Victory Fund	Dem	HR	VA		$702.25	$702.25
Denham, Jeff	NRA Institute for Legislative Action	Rep	HR	CA	$6,628.62		$6,628.62
Dittmar, Jane*	NRA of America Political Victory Fund	Dem	HR	VA		$596.44	$596.44
Faso, John J. Mr.	NRA Institute for Legislative Action	Rep	HR	NY	$34,273.54		$34,273.54
Feingold, Russell*	NRA of America Political Victory Fund	Dem	SE	WI		$73,670.42	$73,670.42
Feingold, Russell Dana*	NRA Institute for Legislative Action	Dem	SE	WI		$180,647.79	$180,647.79
Gallagher, Michael	NRA of America Political Victory Fund	Rep	HR	WI	$1,788.75		$1,788.75
Gallagher, Michael John	NRA Institute for Legislative Action	Rep	HR	WI	$30,844.90		$30,844.90
Garrett, Scott Rep.*	NRA Institute for Legislative Action	Rep	HR	NJ	$21,612.58		$21,612.58
Garrett, Thomas	NRA of America Political Victory Fund	Rep	HR	VA	$902.73		$902.73
Glenn, Darryl*	NRA Institute for Legislative Action	Rep	SE	CO	$1,796.52		$1,796.52

Campaign Expenses Paid by NRA Committees in the 2016 National Elections

Candidate Name	Name	Party	Office	State	Support	Oppose	Totals
					Candidate		
Glenn, Darryl*	NRA of America Political Victory Fund	Rep	SE	CO	$7,866.75		$7,866.75
Goodlatte, Bob	NRA of America Political Victory Fund	Rep	HR	VA	$1,463.19		$1,463.19
Grassley, Charles E Sen	NRA Institute for Legislative Action	Rep	SE	IA	$86,208.31		$86,208.31
Grassley, Chuck	NRA of America Political Victory Fund	Rep	SE	IA	$2,148.29		$2,148.29
Griffith, Morgan	NRA of America Political Victory Fund	Rep	HR	VA	$702.26		$702.26
Guinta, Frank*	NRA Institute for Legislative Action	Rep	HR	NH	$38,270.96		$38,270.96
Hardy, Cresent*	NRA Institute for Legislative Action	Rep	HR	NV	$14,484.33		$14,484.33
Hartzler, Vicky	NRA of America Political Victory Fund	Rep	HR	MO	$694.01		$694.01
Hassan, Margaret Wood	NRA Institute for Legislative Action	Dem	SE	NH		$48,099.66	$48,099.66
Heck, Joe*	NRA Institute for Legislative Action	Rep	SE	NV	$92,798.76		$92,798.76
Heck, Joe*	NRA of America Political Victory Fund	Rep	SE	NV	$8,314.07		$8,314.07
Hudson, Richard	NRA of America Political Victory Fund	Rep	HR	NC	$2,908.00		$2,908.00
Hurd, William	NRA Institute for Legislative Action	Rep	HR	TX	$13,844.13		$13,844.13
Isakson, Johnny	NRA of America Political Victory Fund		HR	GA	$245.74		$245.74
Issa, Darrell	NRA Institute for Legislative Action	Rep	HR	CA	$5,885.66		$5,885.66
Johnson, James	NRA of America Political Victory Fund		HR	LA	$1,601.41		$1,601.41
Johnson, Ron	NRA of America Political Victory Fund	Rep	SE	WI	$94,808.64		$94,808.64

Continued ▶

Campaign Expenses Paid by NRA Committees in the 2016 National Elections

Candidate Name	Name	Candidate			Support	Oppose	Totals
		Party	Office	State			
Johnson, Ronald Harold	NRA Institute for Legislative Action	Rep	SE	WI	$270,762.23		$270,762.23
Jones, Scott*	NRA Institute for Legislative Action	Rep	HR	CA	$7,335.21		$7,335.21
Joyce, David	NRA of America Political Victory Fund	Rep	HR	OH	$4,650.96		$4,650.96
Kander, Jason*	NRA Institute for Legislative Action	Dem	SE	MO		$759,494.53	$759,494.53
Kander, Jason*	NRA of America Political Victory Fund	Dem	SE	MO		$1,855,764.60	$1,855,764.60
Katko, John M	NRA Institute for Legislative Action	Rep	HR	NY	$26,645.44		$26,645.44
Kennedy, John	NRA of America Political Victory Fund	Rep	SE	LA	$123,823.51		$123,823.51
Kitts, Derek*	NRA of America Political Victory Fund	Dem	HR	VA		$702.25	$702.25
Klepinger, Robert*	NRA of America Political Victory Fund	Dem	HR	OH		$599.56	$599.56
Knight, Steve	NRA Institute for Legislative Action	Rep	HR	CA	$7,426.16		$7,426.16
Lahood, Darin	NRA of America Political Victory Fund	Rep	HR	IL	$8,781.07		$8,781.07
Latta, Bob	NRA of America Political Victory Fund	Rep	HR	OH	$777.30		$777.30
Lee, Mike	NRA of America Political Victory Fund	Rep	SE	UT	$161.31		$161.31
Long, Wendy	NRA Institute for Legislative Action	Rep	SE	NY	$3,003.41		$3,003.41
Mast, Brian	NRA Institute for Legislative Action	Rep	HR	FL	$24,705.82		$24,705.82
Masto, Catherine	NRA of America Political Victory Fund	Dem	SE	NV		$688,146.21	$688,146.21
Masto, Catherine Cortez	NRA Institute for Legislative Action	Dem	SE	NV		$3,196,440.61	$3,196,440.61

Campaign Expenses Paid by NRA Committees in the 2016 National Elections

Candidate Name	Name	Candidate					
		Party	Office	State	Support	Oppose	Total
Mccarthy, Kevin	NRA of America Political Victory Fund	Rep	HR	CA	$5,893.07		$5,893.07
Mcsally, Martha E	NRA Institute for Legislative Action	Rep	HR	AZ	$11,204.10		$11,204.10
Mica, John L. Mr.*	NRA Institute for Legislative Action	Rep	HR	FL	$58,265.55		$58,265.55
Mills, Stewart*	NRA Institute for Legislative Action	Rep	HR	MN	$29,274.89		$29,274.89
Mills, Thomas	NRA of America Political Victory Fund	Dem	HR	NC	$599.56		$599.56
Moran, Jerry	NRA Institute for Legislative Action	Rep	SE	KS	$528.94		$528.94
Mowrer, Jim*	NRA of America Political Victory Fund	Dem	HR	IA		$800.57	$800.57
Mullin, Markwayne	NRA of America Political Victory Fund	Rep	HR	OK	$190.47		$190.47
Mundy, Keith*	NRA of America Political Victory Fund	Dem	HR	OH		$599.56	$599.56
Murphy, Christopher S	NRA Institute for Legislative Action	Dem	SE	FL		$34,488.78	$34,488.78
Murphy, Patrick*	NRA of America Political Victory Fund	Dem	SE	FL		$317,551.25	$317,551.25
Murphy, Patrick E*	NRA Institute for Legislative Action	Dem	SE	FL		$1,972,979.45	$1,972,979.45
Nelson, Tom*	NRA of America Political Victory Fund	Dem	HR	WI		$859.59	$859.59
Neu, James*	NRA of America Political Victory Fund	Dem	HR	OH		$599.56	$599.56
Paul, Rand	NRA Institute for Legislative Action	Rep	SE	KY	$70,329.82		$70,329.82
Pittenger, Robert	NRA of America Political Victory Fund	Rep	HR	NC	$817.43		$817.43
Poliquin, Bruce L	NRA Institute for Legislative Action	Rep	HR	ME	$107,922.97		$107,922.97

Continued ▼

Campaign Expenses Paid by NRA Committees in the 2016 National Elections

Candidate Name	Name	Candidate Party	Candidate Office	Candidate State	Candidate Support	Candidate Oppose	Total
Portman, Rob	NRA Institute for Legislative Action	Rep	SE	OH	$345,437.40		$345,437.40
Portman, Rob	NRA of America Political Victory Fund	Rep	SE	OH	$242,148.89		$242,148.89
Renacci, James	NRA of America Political Victory Fund	Rep	HR	OH	$777.30		$777.30
Rosen, Jacky	NRA of America Political Victory Fund	Dem	HR	NV		$872.39	$872.39
Ross, Deborah*	NRA of America Political Victory Fund	Dem	SE	NC		$3,272,114.16	$3,272,114.16
Ross, Deborah K*	NRA Institute for Legislative Action	Dem	SE	NC		$2,315,126.89	$2,315,126.89
Rouzer, David	NRA of America Political Victory Fund	Rep	HR	NC	$217.86		$217.86
Rubio, Marco	NRA Institute for Legislative Action	Rep	SE	FL	$852,572.76		$852,572.76
Rubio, Marco	NRA of America Political Victory Fund	Rep	SE	FL	$61,950.64		$61,950.64
Shelby, Richard	NRA of America Political Victory Fund	Rep	SE	AL	$135,607.29		$135,607.29
Smucker, Lloyd	NRA of America Political Victory Fund	Rep	HR	PA	$147,183.93		$147,183.93
Smucker, Lloyd K	NRA Institute for Legislative Action	Rep	HR	PA	$53,368.71		$53,368.71
Strickland, Ted*	NRA of America Political Victory Fund	Dem	SE	OH		$1,749,236.80	$1,749,236.80
Tarkanian, Danny*	NRA Institute for Legislative Action	Rep	HR	NV	$17,047.83		$17,047.83
Tarkanian, Danny*	NRA of America Political Victory Fund	Rep	HR	NV	$872.42		$872.42
Tenney, Claudia	NRA Institute for Legislative Action	Rep	HR	NY	$37,652.38		$37,652.38
Tipton, Scott R.	NRA Institute for Legislative Action	Rep	HR	CO	$38,908.10		$38,908.10

Campaign Expenses Paid by NRA Committees in the 2016 National Elections

Candidate						
Candidate Name	Name	Party	Office	State	Support	Oppose	Total
Trump, Donald	NRA of America Political Victory Fund	Rep	Pres	US	$1,835,714.01		$1,835,714.01
Trump, Donald J.	NRA Institute for Legislative Action	Rep	Pres	US	$16,670,614.13		$16,670,614.13
Turner, Michael	NRA of America Political Victory Fund	Rep	HR	OH	$777.30		$777.30
Yoder, Kevin	NRA Institute for Legislative Action	Rep	HR	KS	$9,521.07		$9,521.07
Young, David	NRA Institute for Legislative Action	Rep	HR	IA	$39,562.17		$39,562.17
Young, David	NRA of America Political Victory Fund	Rep	HR	IA	$800.58		$800.58
Young, Todd	NRA of America Political Victory Fund	Rep	SE	IN	$233.24		$233.24
Young, Todd Christopher	NRA Institute for Legislative Action	Rep	SE	IN	$391,108.41		$391,108.41
Zeldin, Lee M	NRA Institute for Legislative Action	Rep	HR	NY	$36,138.97		$36,138.97
					$23,480,143.60	$42,845,566.99	$66,325,710.59

FURTHER READING

Adams, Les, *The Second Amendment Primer,* A Citizens Guidebook to the History, Sources, and Authorities for the Constitutional Right to Keep and Bear Arms, Skyhorse Publishing, 1996.

Allen, John, *Gun Control*, Reference point Pr Inc (2018).

Carlson, Jennifer. 2015. *Citizen-Protectors: The Everyday Politics of Guns in an Age of Decline.* New York: Oxford University Press.

Cook, Philip J., and Kristin A. Goss. 2014. *The Gun Debate: What Everyone Needs to Know.* New York: Oxford University Press.

Cornell, Saul, *A Well Regulated Militia*, The Founding Fathers and the origins of gun control in America. Oxford University Press, USA 2008.

Cornell, Saul, Nathan Kozuskanich (Editor), *The Second Amendment on Trial:* Critical Essays on District of Columbia v. Heller, University of Massachusetts Press, 2013.

Cullen, Dave, *Parkland Birth of a Movement.* Harper Collins (2018).

Diaz, Tom, *The Last Gun: How Changes in the Gun Industry are Killing Americans and What it Will Take to Stop It.* The New Press (2013).

Dunbar-Ortiz, Roxanne, *Loaded: A Disarming History of the Second Amendment.* City Lights Books (2018).

Goss, Kristin A. 2006. *Disarmed: The Missing Movement for Gun Control in America.* Princeton, NJ: Princeton University Press.

Hogg, David, *Never Again: A New Generation Draws the Line.* Penguin Random House (2018).

Lerner, Sarah, *Parkland Speaks: Survivors from Marjory Stoneman Douglas Share Their Stories.* Random House (2019).

Lewis, Sinclair. *It Can't Happen Here: A Novel.* New York: Doubleday, 1935.

Lott, John R. *The Bias Against Guns: Why Almost Everything You've Heard About Gun Control is Wrong.* Regnery Publishing (2003).

Melzer, Scott. 2009. *Gun Crusaders: The NRA's Culture War.* New York: New York University Press.

Ludwig, Robert W. "Heller Sequels and 2nd Amendment, Still Undecided: Part 3." Portfolio Media, Inc. New York, August 24, 2017.

Ludwig, Robert W. "Heller Sequels and Second Amendment, Still Undecided: Part 1." Portfolio Media, Inc., New York, July 20, 2017.

Ludwig, Robert W. "Heller Sequels and Second Amendment, Still Undecided: Part 2." Portfolio Media, Inc., New York, August 3, 2017.

Ludwig, Robert W. "The Historic Legal Blunder That Enabled our Gun Epidemic," Portfolio Media. Inc. New York, April 25, 2018.

Miller, David. *Illustrated Directory of 20th Century Guns.* London: Salamander Books Ltd., 2001.

Obert, Jonathan. 2018. *The Six-Shooter State: Public and Private Violence in American Politics.* New York: Cambridge University Press.

Reilly, John Francis, and Barbara A. Braig Allen. *"Political Campaign and Lobbying Activities of IRC 501(c)(4), (c)(5), and (c)(6) Organizations."* Internal Revenue Service Exempt Organizations-Technical Instruction Program for FY 2003. https://www.irs.gov/pub/irs-tege/eotopicl03.pdf.

Russell, Carl P. *Guns on the Early Frontier.* Mineola: Dover Publications, Inc., 2005. Originally published by the University of California Press, Berkeley and Los Angeles, 1957.

Scalia, Antonin, and Bryan A Garner. *Reading Law: The Interpretation of Legal Texts.* St. Paul: Thomson/West, 2012.

Spitzer, Robert. 2018. *The Politics of Gun Control.* 7th ed. New York: Routledge.

Street, Christopher. *Gun Control: Guns in America, The Full Debate.* Create Space Publishing, August 8, 2016. Also available at https:wwwaudible.com/pd/gun control-guns-in-America-the-full-debate.

Steffens, Bradley, *Gun Violence and Mass Shootings.* Reverence Point Pr Inc. (2019)

Stevens, John Paul. *Six Amendments: How and Why We Should Change the Constitution.* New York: Little Brown and Company, 2014.

Tushnet, Mark V. 2007. *Out of Range: Why the Constitution Can't End the Battle Over Guns.* New York: Oxford University Press.

Vizzard, William J. 2000. *Shots in the Dark: The Policy, Politics, and Symbolism of Gun Control.* New York: Rowman & Littlefield.

Waldman, Michael, *The Second Amendment: A Biography.* Simon and Schuster Paperbacks (2014).

Williams, David C. 2003. *The Mythic Meanings of the Second Amendment: Taming Political Violence in a Constitutional Republic.* New Haven, CT: Yale University Press.

Wilson, Harry L. 2015. *The Triumph of the Gun-Rights Argument: Why the Gun Control Debate Is Over.* Santa Barbara, CA: Praeger.

Winkler, Adam. 2013. *Gun Fight: The Battle over the Right to Bear Arms in America.* New York: W.W. Norton and Company.

Additional books, constitutional decisions, statutes, court opinions and newspaper articles appear in the end notes which follow.

ENDNOTES

Introduction

[1] Campbell Robertson, Julie Bosman and Mitch Smith, *New York Times*, August 5, 2019, p. AI.

[2] Nine months following the Walmart shooting at El Paso one of those wounded there, Guillermo Garcia, died after more than 50 operations to save his life bringing the total killed to 23. Manny Fernandez and Sarah Mervosh, "9 Months After El Paso Attack, A Gentle Giant Dies," *New York Times National*, April 28, 2020, p. A17.

[3] *District of Columbia. v. Heller,* 554 U.S. 570, 128 S. Ct. 2783, 171 L. Ed. 2d 637 (2008).

[4] Christina Hall and Kristi Tanner, "Guns in Michigan 'a patchwork of data'." *Detroit Free Press USA Today Network*, August 11, 2019, p. 17A.

[5] *Heller* at 636.

[6] *Id.* at 626.

[7] *Id.* at 635.

[8] *Id.* at 592.

[9] *Id.* at 626.

[10] *Id.* at 639 (Stevens, J., dissenting).

[11] U.S. Department of Justice, Federal Bureau of Investigation, *Crime in the United States, 2016*, (Washington, D.C. 2017), https://ucr.fbi.gov/crime-in-the-u.s/2016/crime-in-the-u.s.-2016/violent-crime.

[12] Julie Turkewitz, Audra D.S. Burch and Liam Stack, "'A Mother Weeps for Her Angel: 'I Hope She Didn't Die for Nothing'," *New York Times*, February 16, 2018, p. A1.

[13] Vivian Yee and Amy Harmon, "Prayers Flood Shaken Town That Has Long Found Solace in Faith," *New York Times*, May 19, 2018, p. A1; Manny Fernandez, Richard Fausset and Jess Bidgood, "17-Year-Old Student Used Father's Guns in the Attack, Officials Say," *New York Times*, May 19, 2018, p. A1.

Chapter 1

[1] The Small Arms Survey is a project of the Graduate Institute of International and Development Studies, Geneva, Switzerland. Chart retrieved from *Small Arms Survey Research Notes* No. 9 September 2011 http://www.smallarmssurvey.org/fileadmin/docs/H-Research_Notes/SAS-Research-Note-9.pdf.

[2] The U.S. Census Bureau reports the population of the United States as 327,711,110 and the population of the world as over 7,472,701,000. https://www.census.gov/popclock/ (accessed May 13, 2018).

[3] The Gun Violence Archive is an independent data collection and research group with no affiliation with any advocacy organization. The not-for-profit corporation was formed in 2013 to provide free online access to accurate infor-

mation about gun-related violence in the United States. Year totals are available online at http://www.gunviolencearchive.org/past-tolls.

4 *Id.* p.32.

5 John Donohue and Theodora Boulota, "That Assault Weapon Ban Worked." *New York Times*, September 5, 2019, p.A27.

6 Audrey Carlsen and Sahil Chinoy, "What It Takes to Buy a Gun in 15 Countries," *New York Times*, March 8, 2018, pp. A14-A15.

7 Nicholas Kristof, "How to Win an Argument About Guns," *New York Times*, April 5, 2018, p. A25.

8 Jacqueline Howard, CNN updated December 14, 2018.

9 Samuel Eliot Morrison, *Oxford History of the American People* (New York: Oxford University Press, 1965), p. 161.

10 Editorial Board, "Moscow's Monument to Murder," *New York Times*, September 21, 2017, p. A26.

11 C.J. Chivers with illustrations by Attila Futaki, "Tools of Modern Terror: How the AK-47 and AR-15 Evolved Into Rifles of Choice for Mass Shootings," *New York Times*, Interactive at https://www.nytimes.com/interactive/2016/world/ak-47-mass-shootings.html.

12 Nathan Koppel, "Putting Guns Out in the Open," *Wall Street Journal*, March 20. 2012, p. A5.

13 If "open carry" is ever combined with "stand your ground," a modern Wyatt Earp will not be able to compel the Clantons to stash their sidearms behind the bar when they come in to shoot up Tombstone.

14 18 U.S.C. §922 (p).

15 Michael D. Shear, Tiffany Hsu and Kirk Johnson, "Judge Presses Pause on the Downloadable Gun." *New York Times*, 8/1/2018, p. A-1. See also "Headlines" *Detroit Free Press*, "Judge blocks online plans for printing untraceable 3D guns, " 8/28/2018 p. 7A.

16 Deirdre Shesgreen and Josh Hafner, "Courts block blueprints for 3-D printable firearms." *USA Today* reprinted in *Detroit Free Press*, August 1, 2018 p. 6A.

17 Mike Householder and Ed White, "ATF traces gun used in Detroit police shooting," *San Diego Union-Tribune*, January 28, 2011, http://www.sandiegouniontribune.com/sdut-atf-traces-gun-used-in-detroit-police-shooting-2011jan26-story.html.

18 Gregory Gibson, "The Parkland Massacre Isn't an Anniversary," *New York Times*, February 14, 2020, p. A27.

19 Richard A. Oppel Jr. "A Rush to Buy Guns, With a Surge of Anxious First-Time Gun Buyers," *New York Times*, March 17, 2020, p. A9.

Chapter 2

1 The Continental Congress adopted the Articles of Confederation, the first constitution, on November 15, 1777. Ratification of the Articles by all 13 states concluded March 1, 1781. The Articles created a loose confederation of sovereign states and a weak central government. The need for a stronger Federal

government led to the Constitutional Convention in 1787. https://www.loc.gov/rr/program/bib/ourdocs/articles.html.

2   Benjamin Franklin reportedly made this response to Mrs. Powel when she asked him outside of Convention Hall to describe the new form of government. Walter Isaacson, *Benjamin Franklin An American Life* (New York: Simon and Shuster, 2003), p. 459.

3   Lincoln spoke these words at the Republican State Convention on June 6, 1858. Paul M. Angle and Earl Schenck Miers, *The Living Lincoln* (New York: Barnes & Noble, 1995), p. 212.

4   *Id.* p. 591.

5   *Marbury v. Madison*, 5 U.S. 137, 163, 2 L.Ed. 60 (1803).

6   *Id.* at 177.

7   Bergen Evans, *Dictionary of Quotations* (New York: Delacourt Press, 1968), p. 378.

8   *See, e.g., U.S. v. Cruikshank*, 92 U.S. 542, 552, 2 Otto 542, 23 L.Ed. 588 (1875).

9   554 U.S. 570, 128 S.Ct. 2783, 171 L. Ed.2d 637 (2008).

10   561 U.S. 742, 130 S.Ct. 3020, 177 L. Ed. 2d 894 (2010).

11   83 U.S. 36, 21 L. Ed.394, 1872 WL 15386 (1872).

12   *Id.* at 79.

13   *Id.* at 78.

14   *Id.* at 80–81.

15   Ch. 188, 16 Stat. 140 (1870).

16   *United States v. Cruikshank*, 92 U.S. at 547.

17   *Id.* at 553.

18   116 U.S. 252, 265, 6 S.Ct. 580, 29 L. Ed. 615 (1886).

19   307 U.S. 174, 59 S.Ct. 816, 83 L.Ed. 1206 (1939).

Chapter 3

1   *District of Columbia. v. Heller*, 554 U.S.570, 639-40 (2008) (Stevens, J., dissenting).

2   *Id.* at 577.

3   *Id.*

4   *Heller*, 554 U.S. at 630.

5   *Id.*

6   *Id.* at 631 (internal quotation marks omitted).

7   558 U.S. 310 (2010).

8   D.C. Code.

9   Justice Scalia authored a book with Bryan A. Garner titled *Reading Law: The Interpretation of Legal Texts* (St. Paul: Thomson/West, 2012), in which he discussed the doctrine of textualism.

10   *Id.* p. 17.

11   William Strunk and E.B. White, *The Elements of Style,* 4th Edition, 2000 and 1979 Allen and Bacon, p.23.

[12] *Id.* pp. 90 and 93.

[13] *Id.* p. 89.

[14] *The American Heritage Dictionary of the English Language*, 4th Edition, Houghton Mifflin Company, 2000. See also William Strunk and E.B. White, *The Elements of Style,* 4th Edition, 2000 and 1979 Allen and Bacon, p. 89.

[15] Tucker's Blackstone Commentaries, by George Tucker, published by William Young Birch, and Abraham Small, No. 17 South Second Street, Philadelphia, Robert Carr Printer (1803). See Volume 1 pp.145–46 and Appendix, Note D, Section 12, ¶8. "The right of self defence (sic) is the first law of nature: in most governments it has been the study of rulers to confine this right within the narrowest limits."

[16] 824 F 3rd 924,939, (9th Cir. 2016).

[17] 896 F 3rd 1044, 2018 W.L.3542985, (9th Cir. 2018).

[18] *Heller,* 554 U.S. at 626–27.

[19] U.S. Const. art. I, § 8.

[20] *Heller,* 554 U.S. at 624.

[21] Carl P. Russell, *Guns on the Early Frontier* (Mineola: Dover Publications, Inc., 2005). Originally published by the University of California Press, Berkley and Los Angeles, 1957.

[22] David Miller, *Illustrated Directory of 20th Century Guns* (London: Salamander Books Ltd., 2001).

[23] *See also* Ken Range, ed., *Gun Digest 2006* (Gun Digest Books, 2005), which similarly describes and illustrates hundreds of handguns, rifles, and shotguns currently available.

[24] *Heller,* 554 U.S. at 629 (quoting *Miller,* 307 U.S. at 179).

[25] *Id.*

[26] *Id.*

[27] *Miller,* 307 U.S. at 178 (internal quotation marks omitted).

[28] *Heller,* 554 U.S. at 622. In his dissent in *Heller,* Justice Stevens disagreed with Justice Scalia's explanation of *Miller.* Stevens wrote, "The view of the Amendment we took in *Miller* — that it protects the right to keep and bear arms for certain military purposes, but that it does not curtail the Legislature's power to regulate the nonmilitary use and ownership of firearms — is both the most natural reading of the Amendment's text and the most faithful to the history of its adoption." *Id.* at 637–38 (Stevens, J., dissenting).

[29] Gary Fields, "Pistol (Glock) Built a Reputation on its Style, Ease of Use," *Wall Street Journal,* January 12, 2011, p. A5.

[30] Justice John Paul Stevens, however, responding to the movement initiated by the Stoneman Douglas students (in an unusual move for a retired Supreme Court Justice), urged repeal of the Second Amendment in an opinion piece. Stevens, John Paul. "John Paul Stevens: Repeal the Second Amendment." *New York Times,* March 28, 2018, at A23.

[31] Dick Anthony Heller, *et. al.* v. District of Columbia (2nd Cir. 2011) 270F. 3rd 1244.

[32] Robert W. Ludwig, "The Historic Legal Blunder That Enabled our Gun Epidemic," Portfolio Media. Inc., New York, April 25, 2018. Other articles by Ludwig include," Heller Sequels and 2nd Amendment, Still Undecided: Part 1," Portfolio Media, Inc., New York, July 20, 2017; "Heller Sequels and 2nd Amendment, Still Undecided: Part 2," Portfolio Media, Inc., New York, August 3, 2017, and "Heller Sequels and 2nd Amendment, Still Undecided: Part 3," Portfolio Media, Inc. New York, August 2, 2017.

[33] Stuart Chase, *The Tyranny of Words* (New York: Harcourt, Brace and Co., 1938).

[34] The quote is from Oliver Wendell Holmes, Jr., Associate Justice of the United States Supreme Court (1902–1932). The full quote also reads: "The law embodies the story of a nation's development through many centuries and cannot be dealt with as if it contained only the axioms and corollaries of a book of mathematics." "Lecture I.—Early Forms of Liability." *The Common Law*, 2000. http://www.gutenberg.org/files/2449/2449-h/2449-h.htm. At another time Holmes also said, "Certainty generally is illusion, and repose is not the destiny of man." "The Path of the Law," 10 *Harv. L. Rev.* 457 (1897).

Chapter 4

[1] Chicago, Ill., Municipal Code § 8-20-040(a) (2009).

[2] *McDonald*, 561 U.S. at 791.

[3] *Id.* at 752–53 (stating that the Seventh Circuit Court of Appeals could find no basis in Supreme Court precedent for incorporating the Second Amendment against the states).

[4] 83 U.S. 36, 21 L.Ed.394 (1872).

[5] *McDonald*, 561 U.S. 535.

[6] *Duncan v. Louisiana*, 391 U.S. 145, 88 S.Ct. 1444, 20 L.Ed.2d 491 (1968).

[7] *Gideon v. Wainwright*, 372 U.S. 335, 83 S.Ct. 792, 9 L.Ed.2d 799 (1963); *Powell v. Alabama*, 287 U.S. 45, 53 S.Ct. 55, 77 L.Ed. 158 (1932).

[8] *Miranda v. Arizona*, 348 U.S. 436, 86 S.Ct. 1602, 16 L.Ed.2d 694 (1966); *Griffin v. California*, 380 U.S. 609, 85 S.Ct. 1229, 14 L. Ed.2d 106 (1965); *Malloy v. Hogan*, 378 U.S. 1, 84 S.Ct. 1489, 12 L.Ed.2d 653 (1964).

[9] *Mapp v. Ohio*, 367 U.S. 643, 81 S.Ct. 1684, 6 L.Ed.2d 1081 (1961).

[10] *McDonald*, 561 U.S. at 780–85.

[11] *Id.* at 791.

[12] *Id.* at 780; *Id.* at 861 (Stevens, J., dissenting).

[13] *Id.* at 806 (Thomas, J., concurring in part and concurring in the judgment).

[14] *Id.* at 806.

[15] *Id.* at 758.

[16] *Slaughter-House Cases,* 83 U.S. at 74.

[17] *McDonald*, 561 U.S. at 812 (Thomas, J., concurring in part and concurring in the judgment).

[18] *Id.* at 855.

[19] *Id.* at 858.

Chapter 5

[1] Ch. 757, 48 Stat. 1236 (1934).

[2] *Id.*

[3] *Id.*

[4] *Haynes v. U.S.*, 390 U.S. 85, 88 S.Ct. 722, 19 L.Ed.2d 923 (1968).

[5] Pub. L. 90–618, sec. 922, 82 Stat. 1213 (1968).

[6] Pub. L. 103–322, 108 Stat. 1796 (1994).

[7] *Id.* at sec. 110102(a).

[8] 18 U.S.C. § 921(a)(28) ("The term 'semiautomatic rifle' means any repeating rifle which utilizes a portion of the energy of a firing cartridge to extract the fired cartridge case and chamber the next round, and which requires a separate pull of the trigger to fire each cartridge.").

[9] 26 U.S.C. § 5845(b) ("The term 'machinegun' means any weapon which shoots, is designed to shoot, or can be readily restored to shoot, automatically more than one shot, without manual reloading, by a single function of the trigger.").

[10] *Id.* at sec. 110102(a)(3).

[11] *Id.* at sec. 110102(a)(2).

[12] *Id.* at sec. 110102(a)(3)(A).

[13] *Id.* at sec. 110106.

[14] *Id.* at sec. 110103(b).

[15] Pub. L. 103–322, sec. 110105, 108 Stat. 1796 (1994).

[16] 18 U.S.C. § 922(a)(4).

[17] Thom Patterson, "Police chief: Suspect bought over 6,000 rounds of ammunition through Internet," CNN, July 21, 2012, https://www.cnn.com/2012/07/20/justice/colorado-shooting-weapons/index.html.

[18] Pub. L. 90–618, sec. 922, 82 Stat. 1213, (1968).

[19] *Id.* at sec. 925.

[20] 26 U.S.C. § 5845(b).

[21] *See below*, notes 28–31.

[22] 511 U.S.600, 602 n.1, 114 S.Ct. 1793, 128 L.Ed.2d 608 (1994).

[23] 969 F. 2d 132, 135, (5th Cir. 1992).

[24] 305 F. 3d 643, 655 (7th Cir 2002).

[25] 978 F. 2d 1112, 1113 (9th Cir. 1992).

[26] 343 F. 3d 743 (5th Cir. 2003).

[27] *Id.* at 745.

[28] Atkins, William. U.S. Patent No. 6,101,918A, "Method and Apparatus for Accelerating the Cyclic Firing Rate of a Semiautomatic Firearm" (Washington, D.C.: U.S. Patent and Trademark Office, 2000).

[29] *Id.*; *see also* Ed Leefeldt, CBS News (Oct. 4, 2017, 5:55 PM), https://www.cbsnews.com/news/bump-fire-stock-ar-15-stephen-paddock-guns-deadlier/.

[30] Cottle, Jeremiah. U.S. Patent No. 8,127,658, "Method of shooting a semiauto-

matic firearm." Assignee: Slide Fire Solutions, Inc. (Moran, Texas) (Washington, D.C.: U.S. Patent and Trademark Office, 2012).

[31] Slide Fire Solutions filed suit against Bump Fire Systems for infringement in 2014. When that litigation settled Bump Fire Systems went out of business. Jacki Billings, "Slide Fire Solutions forces Bump Fire Systems out of business." *Guns.com*, July 24, 2016, http://www.guns.com/2016/07/24/slide-fire-solutions-forces-bump-fire-systems-out-of-business.

[32] The Colt AR-15 . . . is a lightweight 5.56 x 45mm magazine-fed gas operated semiautomatic rifle. Note: it is possible to "bump fire" a semiautomatic rifle even if it has no bump stock attached by holding the rifle with one thumb hooked in a belt loop.

[33] Available at http://www.vpc.org/wp-content/uploads/2017/10/ATF-bump-fire-letter-2010.pdf.

[34] U.S. Patent No. 8,127,658 (2012).

[35] A *New York Times* news article reported that sales at Cottle's "upstart company" had soared to $10 million in its first year, 2010. Patrick McGee, "After a Tragedy in Law Vegas, Tears, and Defiance, in Texas," *New York Times*, October 20, 2017, p. A14.

[36] Lauren Gambino, "Dianne Feinstein introduces Senate gun control bill to ban bump stocks," *Guardian US Edition*, October 5, 2017, https://www.theguardian.com/us-news/2017/oct/04/dianne-feinstein-bump-stocks-senate-gun-control-bill.

[37] Rebecca Shabad, "Proposed bans on bump stocks have stalled in Congress," *CBS News*, November 6, 2017. https://www.cbsnews.com/news/proposed-bans-on-bump-stocks-have-stalled-in-congress.

[38] Federal Register Vol. 83 No. 246 Bureau of Alcohol, Tobacco, Firearms, and Explosives 27 CFR Parts 447, 478, and 479 [Docket No. 2018R–22F; AG Order No. 4367–2018] RIN 1140–AA52 Bump-Stock-Type Devices December 26, 2018.

ATF web page bump stock destruction instructions with diagrams here:

https://www.atf.gov/rules-and-regulations/bump-stocks/how-to-destroy

PDF version of instructions here:

https://www.atf.gov/rules-and-regulations/docs/undefined/bump-fire-stocks-and-devicesady-destruction-diagrams/download

[39] Adam Liptak, "Justices Decline to Halt Ban on Bump Stocks While Lawsuit Moves Ahead," *New York Times* National, March 29, 2019, p. A17.

[40] Timothy Williams, "State Senators in Virginia Reject a Ban On Some Rifles," *New York Times*, February 18, 2020, p. A12.

[41] Neil Vigor, "Virginia's Unlikely Shift to the Left is Evidenced in a Series of New Laws," *New York Times National*, April 15, 2020, p. A21.

[42] Gina Kolata, "Desperate Hour in El Paso . . . Surgeons Describe a Scramble to Save Lives After a Mass Shooting at a Walmart." *New York Times*, August 10, 2019, p.A1.

[43] Pub. L. 103–159, 107 Stat. 1536 (1993) (codified at 18 U.S.C. § 922).

[44] The Brady Handgun Violence Prevention Act (Pub. L. 103–159, 107 Stat. 1536,

enacted November 30, 1993, was named after James Brady, the press secretary to President Ronald Reagan, who was critically wounded when John Hinckley tried to assassinate President Reagan. Commonly called the Brady Act.

[45] John Feinblatt, Guest columnist, "End Senate blockade on gun background checks," *Detroit Free Press*, February 28, 2020, p. 14 A.

[46] Kevin Johnson, "FBI sees rise in firearm background checks," *Detroit Free Press*, November 26, 2019, p. 15A.

[47] Pub. L. 109-92, 119 Stat. 2095 (2005) (codified at 15 U.S.C. § 7901 et seq.).

[48] 15 U.S.C. §§ 7901-03.

[49] Kristin Hussey and Elizabeth Williamson, "Suit Against Gun Maker is Allowed to Continue," *New York Times*, November 13, 2019, p.A3.

[50] H.B. 4706, 99th Leg., Reg. Sess. (Mich. 2017) ("A bill to provide for the issuance of restraining orders prohibiting certain individuals from possessing or purchasing firearms and ordering the seizure of a restrained individual's firearms.")

[51] S.B. 937, 99th Leg., Reg. Sess. (Mich. 2018)("A bill to provide for the issuance of restraining orders prohibiting certain individuals from possessing or purchasing firearms and ordering the seizure of a restrained individual's firearms ..."); S.B. 938, 99th Leg., Reg. Sess. (Mich. 2018)("to provide for the forfeiture of firearms and electro-muscular disruption devices under certain circumstances").

[52] Editorial Board, "There's something states can do about gun violence: 'Red-flag' laws," *Washington Post,* March 1, 2018. https://www.washingtonpost .com/opinions/theres-something-states-can-do-about-gun-violence-red-flag-laws/2018/03/01/22ddf06c-1cc4-11e8-ae5a-16e60e4605f3_story.html? noredirect=on&utm_term=.bdbacc14ae57.

[53] NRA Institute for Legislative Action, *NRA-ILA Compendium of State Firearms Laws* (Fairfax: NRA Institute for Legislative Action, 2010), https://www.nraila. org/articles/20100709/compendium-of-state-firearms-laws; *but see* John S. Vernick and Lisa M. Hepburn, "Description and Analysis of State and Federal Laws Affecting Firearm Manufacture, Sale, Possession and Use, 1970-1999," in *Evaluating Gun Policy*, ed. Jens Ludwig and Phillip J. Cook (Washington, D.C.: Brookings Institution Press, 2003). Their research found the number of laws per state range from one to 13. The most common laws concern mandatory minimum sentencing, dealer background checks, "shall issue" or concealed weapon licensing, dealer licensing, and child access protection. *See also* Michael L. Betsch's report on conservative rebuttal, "Gun Control Group's Statistical Study Called 'A Waste of Time'," *CBS News*, July 7, 2008, https://www. cnsnews.com/news/article/gun-control-groups-statistical-study-called-waste-time (noting that the Vernick-Hepburn study called local ordinances "irrelevant," discounted 20,000 as unsubstantiated, and reported 300 laws for the count).

[54] www,newsweek.com/oregon- becomes- eighth-state-require-background-checks-all-gun-sales-3

[55] https://www.npr.org/2018/03/08/591549278

[56] Wikipedia, Assault weapons legislation in the United States.

[57] Wikipedia, High-capacity magazine ban.

[58] Lauren Hepler, Amy Harmon and Richard A. Oppel Jr., "Boy, 6, and girl, 13, Are Among Victims in Attack at Festival." *New York Times* National, July 30, 2019, p A13.

[59] Patricia Mazzei, "'Gunshine State' Enacts Controls," *New York Times*, March 2018, pp A1 and A16.

[60] S.B. 59, 96th Leg., Reg. Sess. (Mich. 2012).

[61] S.B. 584, 99th Leg., Reg. Sess. (Mich. 2017) ("An act to regulate and license the selling, purchasing, possessing, and carrying of certain firearms, …; to prohibit certain conduct against individuals who apply for or receive a license to carry a concealed pistol.").

[62] Kathleen Gray, "Michigan Bills for concealed guns in schools move forward," *Detroit Free Press*, November 8, 2017, pp. 1A and 13A; *see also* Paul Egan, "Mich. Senate OKs gun bills," *Detroit Free Press*, November 9, 2017, pp. 4A and 12A.

[63] *Id.*

[64] Sheryl Gay Stolberg and Erica L. Green, "Not Gun Control, but Alarms, Cameras and Bulletproof Doors," *New York Times*, March 8, 2018, p. A14.

[65] Tom Jackman, "Police chiefs implore Congress not to pass concealed-carry reciprocity gun law," *Washington Post*, April 19, 2018, https://www.washingtonpost.com/news/true-crime/wp/2018/04/19/nations-police-chiefs-implore-congress-not-to-pass-concealed-carry-reciprocity-gun-law/?noredirect=on&utm_term=.8d3bd92404c1.

[66] *See* National Center for Education Statistics, "Table 216.20 Number and enrollment of public, elementary and secondary schools by school level, type and charter and magnet states 1990 -15," https://nces.ed.gov/programs/digest/d16/tables/dt16_216.20.asp; Council for American Private Education, "Private School Statistics at a Glance, PK-12 Enrollment and # of Schools (2013–14.)" http://www.capenet.org/facts.html.

[67] Erica L. Green, "Devos Weighs Funding Guns for Educators," *New York Times*, August 24, 2018, p. A1

Chapter 6

[1] Alexandra Berzon, John R. Emshwiller and Robert A. Guth, "Postings of a Troubled Mind," *Wall Street Journal*, January 12, 2011, pp. A1 and A4.

[2] Sarah Garrecht Gassen and Timothy Williams. "Before Attack, Parents of Tucson Gunman Tried to Address Son's Strange Behavior," *New York Times*, March 28, 2018.3, p. A14.

[3] *World Almanac and Book of Facts*, 2011 Ed. New York: World Almanac Books, 2010, p.179.

[4] Suzette Hackney, "Living with murder," *Detroit Free Press*, November 13, 2011 p. A1.

[5] Joe Gullen and Gina Kaufman, "Is Detroit Ready for a Catastrophe," *Detroit Free Press*, August 25, 2019, p. 1A.

[6] Statistics on Detroit and Chicago homicides and shooting deaths are available on the Internet. *See* Francesca Mirable and Daniel Nass, "What's the Homicide

Capital of America? Murder Rates in U.S. Cities, Ranked.," *The Trace*, https:// www.thetrace.org/2018/04/highest-murder-rates-us-cities-list/.

[7] Christine Hauser, "Chicago Reels as 3 Children Are Gunned Down in 4 Days," *New York Times,* February 16, 2017, p. A19.

[8] Free Press News services, "Gang violence in Chicago: 13 shot to death over holiday weekend," *Detroit Free Press*, September 7, 2016, p. 2A.

[9] Aamer Madhani, "Chicago Suffers Bloody Weekend," *Detroit Free Press*, August 8, 2018, p. 6A.

[10] According to this mlive.com report ("50 largest U.S. cities in 2018 and their population trend since 1950" Julie Mack, June 5, 2019), Baltimore now has almost the same population as Detroit and counts as a "major city":

Chicago, Illinois: 2,705,994

Philadelphia, Pennsylvania: 1,584,138

Dallas, Texas: 1,345,047

El Paso, Texas: 682,669

Detroit, Michigan: 672,662

Baltimore, Maryland: 602,495

Tucson, Arizona: 545,975

https://expo.mlive.com/news/g66l-2019/06/e47df3a99e5816/50-largest-us-cities-in-2018-and-their-population-trend-since-1950.html

[11] U.S. Department of Justice, Federal Bureau of Investigation. *Crime in the United States, 2015.* (Washington, D.C. 2016), https://ucr.fbi.gov/crime-in-the-u.s/2015/crime-in-the-u.s.-2015.

[12] Alan Blinder and Timothy Williams, "Dallas Gunman Planned Larger Attack, Chief Says," *New York Times*, July 11, 2016, pp. A1 and A16.

[13] Niraj Chokshi, "Deaths in the Line of Duty," *New York Times*, July 28, 2016, p. A17.

[14] Sharon LaFraniere and Daniela Porat, "When Bullets Hit Bystanders," *New York Times*, June 10, 2016, p. A20.

[15] Larry Buchanan et al, "Comparing the Las Vegas Attack with Daily Gun Deaths in U.S. Cities," *New York Times*, October 9, 2017, p. A16.

[16] Edgar Sandoval, "As Gang-Related Shootings Surge, a Plea: 'Stop the Bleeding,'" *New York Times*, December 6, 2019, p.A25.

[17] Tim Arango, "Gunfire Erupts in Several Cities as 2020 Get Off to a Deadly Start," *New York Times*, January 2, 2020, p. A12.

[18] Links list of articles and reports on firearms suicide.

https://scholar.google.com/scholar?hl=en&as_sdt=0%2C23&as_vis=1&q=gun+suicide+research+united+states&btnG= Links list of research on guns and domestic violence

https://scholar.google.com/scholar?q=gun+domestic+violence+research+united+states&hl=en&as_sdt=0&as_vis=1&oi=scholart

[19] Madeline Drexler, "Guns & Suicide The Hidden Toll," *Harvard Public Health.* https://www.hsph.harvard.edu/magazine/magazine_article/guns-suicide/.

[20] Jacqueline Howard, CNN updated December 14, 2018.

[21] Paper. Violence Policy Center, Research, Investigation, Analysis and Advocacy for a Safer America, 2019.

[22] Emily Cochrane, "Overhaul of Domestic Violence Bill Advances." *New York Times*, April 5, 2019, p. A14. Maureen Groppe, "House renews law to cut domestic violence." USA Today printed in *Detroit Free Press* April 5, 2019, p. 6A.

Chapter 7

[1] *A Tale of Two Cities*, first published 1859 by Charles Dickens.

[2] *Heller*, 554 U.S. 570.

[3] Jennifer Medina, "Revealing Details of Las Vegas Attack, Police Say an Arrest is Likely," *New York Times*, January 20, 2018, p. A18.

[4] Gina Kolata and C.J. Chivers, "Wounds from Military-Style Rifles? 'A Ghastly Thing to See'," *New York Times*, March 4, 2018, https://www.nytimes.com/2018/03/04/health/parkland-shooting-victims-ar15.html.

[5] Associated Press, "New photographs of Las Vegas shooter's room show more of Stephen Paddock's deadly arsenal," *Telegraph*, January 19, 2018, https://www.telegraph.co.uk/news/2018/01/19/new-photographs-las-vegas-shooters-room-released-part-preliminary.

[6] Violent Crime Control and Law Enforcement Act of 1994, Pub. L. 103–322, sec. 110102(a)(v)(1), 108 Stat. 1796 (1994) (amending Gun Control Act of 1968, Pub. L. 90–618, 82 Stat. 1213 (1968)).

[7] Pub. L. 103–322, sec. 110103(a)(w)(1), 108 Stat. 1796.

[8] Pub. L. 103–322, sec. 110102(a)(2), 108 Stat. 1796.

[9] Pub. L. 103–322, sec. 110106, 108 Stat. 1796.

[10] Pub. L. 103–322, sec. 110102(a)(3)(C), 108 Stat. 1796.

[11] Pub. L. 103–322, sec. 110105, 108 Stat. 1796.

[12] Richard A. Oppel, Jr., "Hotel Agrees to Settlement Over Massacre in Las Vegas," *New York Times*, October 4, 2019, p. A12.

Chapter 8

[1] Rachel Philofsky, "D.C. sniper attacks of 2002." Last updated November 10, 2016. *Britannica.com*. https://www.britannica.com/topic/Washington-DC-sniper-attacks-of-2002.

[2] Lloyd Vries, "Ohio Highway Shooter Pleads Guilty" *CBS News*, August 9, 2005, https://www.cbsnews.com/news/ohio-highway-shooter-pleads-guilty/2/.

[3] This Day in History, "Virginia Tech shooting leaves 32 dead," April 16, 2007, https://www.history.com/this-day-in-history/massacre-at-virginia-tech-leaves-32-dead.

[4] CNN Library, "Colorado Theater Shooting Fast Facts," *CNN*, November 30, 2017, https://www.cnn.com/2013/07/19/us/colorado-theater-shooting-fast-facts/index.html.

[5] William Saletan, "Armored and Dangerous," *Slate*, July 23, 2012, http://www.slate.com/articles/health_and_science/human_nature/2012/07/the_aurora_shooting_bulletproof_vests_swat_gear_and_body_armor_refute_the_nra_.html.

[6] Michael D. Shear and Michael S. Schmidt, "12 Shot to Death by Lone Gunman at Capital Base," *New York Times*, September 17, 2013, pp. A1 and A14.

[7] Editorial Board, "Congress Says, Let the Mentally Ill Buy Guns," *New York Times*, February 16, 2017, p. A26.

[8] Alexander Burns, "The Latest Eruption in a Grim Ritual of Rage and Blame," *New York Times*, June 15, 2017.

[9] David Montgomery, Richard A. Oppel Jr. and Jose A. Del Real, "Air Force Error Allowed Texas Gunman to Buy Weapons," *New York Times*, November 7, 2017, p. A1.

[10] Sabrina Tavernise, Amy Harmon and Maya Salam, "Gunman Attacks a Newsroom in Maryland Killing 5 people." *New York Times* June 29, 2018, p. A-1.

[11] Jose A. Del Real, Jennifer Medina and Tim Arango, "13 Dead in California Rampage" *New York Times*, November 9, 2018, page A-1, and Jennifer Medina, Dave Philipps and Serge F. Kovaleski, "Dueling Images: A Smiling Young Marine and a Killer Dressed in Black," *New York Times*, November 9, 2018, page A-21.

[12] Ryan W. Miller, "Police halt 3 mass shooting plots around US," *USA Today* printed in *Detroit Free Press*, August 20, 2019, p. 13A.

[13] Campbell Robertson, Julie Bosman and Mitch Smith, "One Shooting Massacre Follows Another, Shaking a Bewildered Nation to Its Core," *New York Times*, August 5, 2019, p. A1.

[14] Lucinda Holt and Manny Fernandez, "Shooting Spree Across 15 Miles in West Texas Killed 7 and Terrorized 2 Towns." *New York Times*, September 2, 2019, p. A15.

[15] Kalyn Wolfe, Patricia Mazzei, Eric Schmitt and Christine Hauser, "Saudi Pilot Trainee Kills Three in Rampage at Navy Air Base in Florida," *New York Times*, December 7, 2019, p. A-1. Manny Fernandez, "Attacks, Just Days Apart, Reflect Rising Tide of Gun Violence on Military Bases," *New York Times*, December 7, 2019, p. A-17.

[16] John Bacon, "Gunman killed by parishioners," *Detroit Free Press*, December 30, 2019, p. 9A. Patrick McGee and Mihir Zaveri, "'This Would Have Been a Massacre' if Not for Church Security," *New York Times*, December 30, 2019 p. A9.

[17] Johnny Diaz, "Missouri Shooter Kills 4, Including Police Officer," *New York Times*, March 17, 2020, p. A19.

[18] Lisa Marie Pane, "US mass killings hit new high in 2019," *Detroit Free Press*, December 29, 2019, p. 17A.

[19] Michael Gold, "Rampage in Jersey City Was 'Domestic Terrorism,' Officials Say," *New York Times*, December 13, 2019, p. A25.

[20] *Detroit Legal News* posting of February 3, 2020, "Keeping guns away from potential mass shooters" from MSU Today.

Chapter 9

[1] Dave Cullen, "The Depressive and the Psychopath: At last we know why the

Columbine killers did it," *Slate*, April 20, 2004, http://www.slate.com/articles/news_and_politics/assessment/2004/04/the_depressive_and_the_psychopath.html.

2   Gary Stoller and John Bacon, "Details of Newtown shootings released." *Detroit Free Press*, March 29, 2013, p. 2A.

3   Alan Blinder and Daniel Victor, "A School Attack Every Other Day," *New York Times*, January 24, 2018, pp. A1 and A18.

4   Nicholas Kristof, "Mr. Trump, Here's a Hero; It's Your Turn!" *New York Times*, March 8, 2018, p. A27.

5   The *New York Times* published an article on the use of armed guards in our schools. It told of a uniformed, female Sheriff's deputy in the schools in Auburn, Alabama. The deputy carried a sidearm, wore a bulletproof vest and kept an AR-15 stored nearby. Stephanie Saul, Timothy Williams and Anemona Hartocollis, "Hugs, Smiles and a Pistol at the Ready," *New York Times*, March 5, 2018, p. A1.

6   Hasan Dudar, "Large crowd checks out weekend gun show in Novi," *Detroit Free Press*, February 25, 2018, pp 4A-5A.

7   Darcy Schleifstein, Zachary Doughtery and Sarah Emily Braun, "We Won't Let the N.R.A. Win," *New York Times*, March 14, 2018 p. A23; *see also* Editorial Board, "We Stand with the Students," *New York Times*, March 14, 2018, p. A22.

8   Jim Dwyer and Myah Ward, "He Was Shot 3 Times but Never Stopped Charging", *New York Times* National, May 7, 2019, p A12.

9   Patricia Mazzei, "Fight if You Must: Students Take Front-Line Role in Attacks," *New York Times* National, May 10, 2019 p. A13.

10 Weiyi Cai and Jugal K. Patel, "A Half Century of School Schools," *New York Times* National, May 14, 2019.

11 Markham, Edwin, "Outwitted", Modern American Poetry- Modern British Poetry Combined Edition, Edited by Louis Untermeyer, Harcourt, Brace and Company, Fourth Revised Edition, page 10;. Modern American Poetry copyright 1919, 1921, 1925, and 1930 and Modern British Poetry copyright 1920, 1925, and 1930.

12 Cory Colyer, "W. I. Thomas and the Forgotten Four Wishes: A Case Study in the Sociology of Ideas," *American Sociologist* 46, no. 2 (June 2015): p. 248. 2015, https://doi.org/10.1007/s12108-014-9251-8, abstract available at https://link.springer.com/article/10.1007/s12108-014-9251-8.

13 Frank Witsil, "Lawsuit could test Dick's, Walmart gun policy changes," *Detroit Free Press*, March 7, 2018, p. 10A.

14 Headlines, *Detroit Free Press*, April 20, 2018, p. 12A.

15 Headlines, *Detroit Free Press*, June 13, 2018, p. 8A.

16 Michael Corkery, "Walmart to Curtail Its Sales of Ammo." *New York Times National*, September 4, 2019, p. B1.

17 Meg Wagner and Veronica Rocha, "President Trump speaks at NRA convention," CNN, May 7, 2018, https://www.cnn.com/politics/live-news/trump-nra-speech/h_f1ff3a22e7a228d3ec35ab24d58f333f.

18 Rick Jervis of *USA Today*, "Gun-Control Activists flood NRA convention," *Detroit Free Press*, May 5, 2018, p. 6A.

Chapter 10

[1] "Oklahoma City bombing," Wikipedia, https://en.wikipedia.org/wiki/Oklahoma_City_bombing.

[2] "Boston Marathon bombing," Wikipedia, https://en.wikipedia.org/wiki/Boston_Marathon_ bombing.

[3] Adam Nagourney, Ian Lovett, and Richard Pérez-Peña, "California Rampage Leaves Chaos and Death: at Least 14 Killed," *New York Times*, December 3, 2015, pp. A1 and A22.

[4] Jennifer Medina, Richard Pérez-Peña, and Laurie Goodstein, "Arms Stockpile Is Found in Home of Two Suspects," *New York Times*, December 4, 2015, p. A1.

[5] Matthew Haag, "Gunman, Thought to Be Targeting Whites, Kills 3 in Fresno, Police Say," *New York Times*, April 19, 2017, p. A20.

[6] William K. Rashbaum, Alan Feuer, and Adam Goldman, "A Fervent Backer of Trump is Seized in Pipe Bomb Spree," *New York Times*, October 27, 2018, page A1.

[7] Campbell Robertson, Sabrina Tavernise, and Sandra E. Garcia, "Quiet Day at a Synagogue Was Shattered by Gunfire,"*New York Times*, October 29, 2018, p. A1.

[8] Mark Leibovich, "A Massacre in El Paso Turned Gun Violence into O'Rourke's Priority." *New York Times*, September 24, 2019, page A20.

[9] Adeel Hassan, "Assaults Linked to Hate Crimes Were Up in 2018, According to F.B.I.," *New York Times*, November 13, 2019, p. A14.

[10] Michael Gold, "Rampage in Jersey City Was 'Domestic Terrorism,' Officials Say," *New York Times*, December 13, 2019, p. A25.

Chapter 11

[1] 18 U.S.C. §§ 921–31.

[2] 18 U.S.C. § 922.

[3] 18 U.S.C. § 922(q)(2)(A).

[4] Crime Control Act of 1990, Pub. L. 101–647, sec. 1702, 104 Stat. 4789 (1990) (codified at 18 U.S.C. § 922(q)).

[5] 514 U.S. 549, 115 S.Ct. 1624, 131 L. Ed. 626 (1995).

[6] 2 F. 3d 1342 (1993).

[7] 514 U.S. at 558.

[8] *Lopez*, 514 U.S. 567, "The possession of a gun in a local school zone is in no sense an economic activity that might, through repetition elsewhere, substantially affect any sort of interstate commerce."

[9] 521 U.S. 898, 117 S.Ct. 2365, 138 L. Ed. 2d 914 (1997).

[10] *Id.*

Chapter 12

[1] U.S. Const. art. I, § 8.

[2] 293 U.S. 245, 55 S.Ct. 197, 79 L. Ed. 343 (1934).

[3] *Id.* at 263.

[4] Pub. L. No. 37-130, 12 Stat. 503, (1862) (codified at 7 U.S.C. §§ 301–08).

[5] 7 U.S.C. § 304.

[6] Aug. 27, 1928, 46 Stat. 2343, 94 L.N.T.S. 57, 2 BEVANS 73.

[7] 166 N.W. 181 (Minn. 1918).

[8] 202 N.W. 191 (Wis. 1925).

[9] U.S. Const. art. 1, § 8, cl. 12, 15–16.

[10] 197 U.S. 11, 29, 25 S.Ct. 358, 362, 40 L. Ed. 643 (1905).

[11] Ch. 196, 32 Stat. 775 (1903) (also known as "Efficiency in Militia Act of 1903" or the "Dick Act").

[12] *Id.*

[13] 10 U. S. Code § 2576 et.seq.

[14] Defense Logistics Agency Law Enforcement Support Office https://www.dla.mil/DispositionServices/Offers/Reutilization/LawEnforcement/.

"The Law Enforcement Support Office (LESO) or LESO Program, facilitates 10 US Code 2576a, which originated from the National Defense Authorization Act of Fiscal Year 1997."

[15] Frances Tilney Burke, "Remind us: What exactly is the National Guard?" *The Conversation*, April 9, 2018 Updated April 10, 2018 https://theconversation.com/remind-us-what-exactly-is-the-national-guard-94621.

Chapter 13

[1] Quinnipiac University, "February 20, 2018, U.S. Support for Gun Control Tops 2-1, Highest Ever, Quinnipiac University National Poll Finds; Let Dreamers Stay, 80 Percent of Voters Say" https://poll.qu.edu/national/release-detail?ReleaseID=2521.

[2] Megan Brenan, "Support for Stricter Gun Laws Edges Up in U.S.," *Gallup*, October 16, 2017, http://news.gallup.com/poll/220595/support-stricter-gun-laws-edges.aspx.

[3] Mark Abadi, "70 percent of Americans want stricter assault weapon laws — more than ever before," *Business Insider*. February 22, 2018. http://www.businessinsider.com/assault-weapons-ban-poll-gun-reform-2018-2.

[4] Department of Health and Human Services Appropriations Act, 1997, Part of Omnibus Consolidated Appropriations Act, 1997, Pub. L. No. 104-208, 110 Stat. 3009 (1996).

[5] Vanessa Romo, "Bump Stock Manufacturer Is Shutting Down Production," *The Two-Way, National Public Radio*, April 18, 2018, https://www.npr.org/sections/thetwo-way/2018/04/18/603623834/bump-stock-manufacturer-is-shutting-down-production.

[6] In a stunning graphic published the day following the mass shooting at a high school in Santa Fe, Texas, on May 18, 2018, the *New York Times* listed mass shooting per month since the December 2012, Sandy Hook massacre and compared it to Congressional inaction. The data reported show that 1,705 mass shootings occurred in that period (defined as one involving four or more peo-

ple killed or injured in a single event at the same time and location) and that only a single bill (to improve record reporting) was passed during that period. Editorial Board. "How Congress Has Dithered as the Innocent Get Shot," *New York Times*, May 19, 2018, p A20.

[7] This number, which includes suicide victims, exceeds the 1.3 million that have died in "all the wars in American history." Nicholas Kristof, "How to Win an Argument About Guns," *New York Times*, April 5, 2018, p. A25.

[8] Within six weeks of the Stoneman Douglas massacre there were alleged to be more than 763 bomb or gun threats or both at the nation's schools. Kelly Virella and Josephine Sedgwick, "This Is Not a Drill," *New York Times*, March 29, 2018 p. A17.

[9] Ryan Sit, "How Big Is the NRA? Gun Group's Membership Might Not Be as Powerful as It Says," *Newsweek*, March 30, 2018, http://www.newsweek.com/nra-membership-5-million-members-analysis-842040.

[10] Michael S. Rosenwald, "The NRA once believed in gun control and had a leader who pushed for it," *Washington Post*, October 5, 2017, https://www.washington-post.com/news/retropolis/wp/2017/10/05/the-forgotten-nra-leader-who-despised-the-promiscuous-toting-of-guns/?noredirect=on&utm_term=.b195c88a2af3.

[11] U.S. Department of the Treasury. Internal Revenue Service. "Social Welfare Organizations" (Page Last Reviewed or Updated: August 27, 2017), https://www.irs.gov/charities-non-profits/other-non-profits/social-welfare-organiza-tions; *see also* John Francis Reilly and Barbara A. Braig Allen, "Political Campaign and Lobbying Activities of IRC 501(c)(4), (c)(5), and (c)(6) Organizations," Internal Revenue Service Exempt Organizations-Technical Instruction Program for FY 2003, https://www.irs.gov/pub/irs-tege/eotopicl03.pdf.

[12] Pub. L. 109-92, 119 Stat. 2095 (2005) (codified at 15 U.S.C. § 7901 et seq.).

[13] Arica L. Coleman, "When the NRA Supported Gun Control," *Time*, July 29, 2016, http://time.com/4431356/nra-gun-control-history/.

[14] Joel Achenbach, Scott Higham and Sari Horwitz, "How NRA's true believers converted a marksmanship group into a mighty gun lobby," *Washington Post,* January 12, 2013, https://www.washingtonpost.com/politics/how-nras-true-believers-converted-a-marksmanship-group-into-a-mighty-gun-lobby/2013/01/12/51c62288-59b9-11e2-88d0-c4cf65c3ad15_story.html?noredirect=on&utm_term=.ea84308dcc0f.

[15] Pub. L. 109-92, 119 Stat. 2095 (2005) (codified at 15 U.S.C. § 7901 et seq.).

[16] NRA Political Victory Fund, "NRA Releases Grades & Endorsements for June 12 Nevada Primary Election," *nrapvf.org*, May 25, 2018, https://www.nrapvf.org/articles/20180525/nra-releases-grades-endorsements-for-june-12-nevada-primary-election.

[17] Jonathan Martin, "NRA plans $40M fall blitz targeting Obama," *Politico.com*, June 30, 2008, https://www.politico.com/story/2008/06/nra-plans-40m-fall-blitz-targeting-obama-011452.

[18] Daniel Arkin, "Two Colorado lawmakers who backed strict gun control laws ousted in recall," *NBC News*, November 2, 2015, https://www.nbcnews.com/news/us-news/two-colorado-lawmakers-who-backed-strict-gun-control-laws-oust-ed-flna8C11121858.

[19] Kristin Hussey and Rick Rojas, "Gun Maker's Bankruptcy Stalls a Lawsuit Brought by Newtown Families," *New York Times*, April 2, 2018, p. A19.

[20] Megan Wilson, "The NRA's power: By the numbers," *The Hill*, October 8, 2017 http://thehill.com/business-a-lobbying/business-a-lobbying/354317-the-nras-power-by-the-numbers.

[21] NRA Civil Rights Defense Fund, "Eligible Cases," https://www.nradefensefund.org/eligible-cases.aspx.

[22] Megan Wilson, "The NRA's power: By the numbers," *The Hill*, October 8, 2017 http://thehill.com/business-a-lobbying/business-a-lobbying/354317-the-nras-power-by-the-numbers.

[23] Snopes.com, "Fact Check: Is the NRA a Tax-Exempt Nonprofit Organization?" February 23, 2018. https://www.snopes.com/fact-check/nra-tax-exempt-non-profit/.

[24] *Id.*

[25] Alana Abramson, "Membership in Gun Groups Is Spiking After the Florida Shooting," *Time*, March 2, 2018, http://time.com/5176471/national-rifle-association-membership-florida-shooting/.

[26] Jennifer Steinhauer, "Upstart Group Pushes Harder Than the N.R.A.," *New York Times*, April 3, 2013, p. A1.

[27] Center for Responsive Politics, "Gun Owners of America Profile for All Election Cycles," https://www.opensecrets.org.

[28] Center for Responsive Politics, "Gun Rights: Long-Term Contribution Trends," https://www.opensecrets.org/industries/totals.php?cycle=2018&ind=Q13.

[29] *Id.*

[30] 17 U.S. 518, 4 Wheat. 518, 4 L. Ed. 629 (1819).

[31] *Id.* at 636.

[32] Editors of Encyclopaedia Britannica, "Dartmouth College case," Last updated April 5, 2017, https://www.britannica.com/event/Dartmouth-College-case.

[33] 435 U.S. 765, 778 n.14, 98 S.Ct. 1407, 55 L.Ed.2d 707 (2000).

[34] 540 U.S. 93, 203-09, 124 S.Ct. 619, 157 L.Ed.2d 491 (2003).

[35] 494 U.S. 652, 110 S.Ct. 1391, 108 L.Ed.2d 652 (1990).

[36] *Id.* at 660.

[37] Pub. L. 107–155, 116 Stat. 81, (2002) (also known as McCain-Feingold Act).

[38] 2 U.S.C. § 434(f)(3)(A).

[39] 2 U.S.C. § 441b(b)(2).

[40] 558 U.S. 310, 130 S.Ct. 876, 175 L.Ed.2d 753 (2010).

[41] 494 U.S. 652 (1990).

[42] 540 U.S 93, 203-09, (2003).

[43] *Citizens United*, 558 U.S. at 340.

[44] *Id.* at 443 (Stevens, J., dissenting).

[45] *Id.* at 447–48.

[46] *Id.* at 450.

[47] *Id.* at 452–53.

[48] *Id.* at 455.

[49] *See* http://www.opensecrets.org/industries/indus.php?ind=Q13.

[50] 572 U.S. p. 185, 134 S.Ct. 1434, 188 L.Ed.2d 468 (2014).

[51] 424 U.S. 1, 96 S.Ct. 612, 46 L.Ed.2d 659 (1976).

[52] *McCutcheon*, 134 S.Ct. at 1449.

[53] http://www.opensecrets.org/industries/indus. See also FEC statistics for donors: https://www.fec.gov/data/advanced/?tab=spending.

[54] 60 U.S. 393, 15 L.Ed. 691 (1857).

[55] Congress renames the nation "United States of America," https://www.history.com/this-day-in-history/congress-renames-the-nation-united-states-of-america (original post Sep 1, 2010, updated Sep 5, 2019).

[56] Kevin McCoy, "Bank of America Halts Lending to Some Gunmakers," *Detroit Free Press*, April 12, 2018, p. 4B.

[57] Alex Gangitano and Scott Wong, "Here are the gun policies for America's largest retailers," *The Hill*, September 7, 2019.

[58] David Yaffe-Bellany and AmieTsang, "Sales Plunge So Gun Unit Will Spin Off," *New York Times*, November 15, 2019, p. 81.

[59] Danny Hakim and Zach Montague, "Ad Firm Sues in Response to Lawsuit from N.R.A.," *New York Times* National, May 24, 2019, p. A19.

[60] Danny Hakim, "N.R.A. Citing Attempt to Oust Chief, Suspends its 2nd Highest Official", *New York Times* National, June 21, 2019, p._ . Also, Danny Hakim, N.R.A. Shuts Down Production of NRATV As Its No.2 Official Resigns," *New York Times* National, June 27, 2019, p. A20.

[61] Danny Hakim, "Wealthy Donor Marshals Forces to Target Leader of N.R.A." *New York Times* National, July 3, 2019, p. A1.

[62] Danny Hakim, "N.R.A. Faces New Scrutiny Over Actions of its Charity," *New York Times*, July 13, 2019, p. A10.

[63] Maggie Astor and Weiyi Cai, "The N.R.A. Clout Is Following Its Allies in Congress Out the Door," *New York Times*, August 27, 2019, p. A11, and Maggie Astor, "Quantifying the Influence of the N.R.A.," *New York Times*, August 27, 2019, p. A2. The latter news article explains how the underlying data was collected based on six election cycles.

[64] Maggie Astor, "Defeat in 2013 Gave Gun-Control Groups Activists a Base to Work From," *New York Times* National, April 17, 2019 p. A17.

Chapter 14

[1]   Alex Kingsbury, Editorial Observer, "It's Too Late to Ban Assault Weapons," *New York Times*, August 17, 2019, p. A22.

[2]   Kristen Jordan Shamus, "American Anxiety: Fear of Mass Shootings Grows," *Detroit Free Press*, *USA Today* Network, August 11, 2019, p. 1A and 18A. Dan Rivera, "Amnesty International Has Issued a Travel Warning For The U.S. Due To Gun Violence." https://uproxx.com/news/2019/08/08-amnesty travel warning-us-2019.

[3]   Claire Parker, "Gun violence in America prompts Amnesty International and a

growing list of countries to issue travel warnings," Washington Post, August 7, 2019. https://beta.washingtonpost.com/world/2019/08/06/gun-violence-amer-ica-prompts-growing-list-countries-issue-travel-warnings/?noredirect=on.

4   Gary Wills, *Lincoln at Gettysburg* (New York: Simon & Schuster, 1992), p.263.

5   John Paul Stevens, "John Paul Stevens: Repeal the Second Amendment." *New York Times*, March 28, 2018, p. A23. See also, Stevens, John Paul: *Six Amendments: How and Why We Should Change the Constitution.* New York: Little Brown and Company, 2014, p. 125.

6   U.S. National Archives and Records Administration. Bill of Rights Center for Legislative Archives National Archives and Records Administration, "Handout 2: James Madison's Proposed Amendments to the Constitution, June 8, 1789," https://www.archives.gov/files/legislative/resources/education/bill-of-rights/images/handout-2.pdf; *See also* Chi Luu, "Revisiting the Messy Language of the second Amendment," *JSTOR Daily*, April 4, 2018, https://daily.jstor.org/revisiting-messy-language-second-amendment/.

7   *Heller*, 554 U.S. at 635.

8   U.S. Constitution, Art. III, Sec. 1.

9   Adam Liptak, "After 10 Years, Justices Are Poised to Break Silence on Gun Rights," *New York Times*, December 2, 2019, p. A13. See also, Editorial, "The Justices Should Drop This Case," *New York Times*, December 4, 2019, p. A24.

10   Associated Press, "Build-your-own AR-15 rifle class provokes backlash," *Detroit Free Press*, March 29, 2018, p. 7A.

11   Catie Edmondson, "House Passes First Major Gun Control Law in Decades," *New York Times*, 2/28/2019, p. A-21.

12   Maureen Groppe, U.S.A, "House passes bill extending time for gun background checks," *New York Times*, 3/1/2019, p. 3A.

13   *Kolbe v. Hogan*, 849 F.3d 114, 121 (4th Cir. 2017).

14   *Id., cert. denied*, 138 S.Ct. 469, November 27, 2017.

15   *Worman v. Healey*, Case 1:17-cv-10107-WGY, 2018 WL 1663445 (D. Mass., April 5, 2018) (holding that the firearms and large magazines Massachusetts had banned are "not within the scope of the personal right to 'bear Arms' under the Second Amendment,"); *see also* Alanna Durkin Richer, "Federal Judge Upholds Massachusetts Assault Weapons Ban," *WBUR News*, April 06, 2018, Updated April 07, 2018, http://www.wbur.org/news/2018/04/06/judge-upholds-massachusetts-weapons-ban.

16   Lori Higgins, "Court Upholds School Ban," *Detroit Free Press*, July 28, 2018, p. 1A.

17   Concealed Carry Reciprocity Act of 2017, H.R. 38, 115th Cong. (2017); *see* Daniel Webster, "Gun owners and Republicans don't really want concealed carry reciprocity bill," *The Hill*, December 20, 2017. http://thehill.com/blogs/congress-blog/politics/365543-gun-owners-and-republicans-dont-really-want-concealed-carry.

18   Library of Congress, Law Library of Congress, "Firearms-Control Legislation and Policy: Australia," Last Updated July 30, 2015, http://www.loc.gov/law/help/firearms-control/Australia.php.

[19] Richard Perez-Pena. "Extremist Hate Fuels New Zealand Massacre: 49 Killed at Mosques. Australian Charged in a Spree Calculated to Reverberate." New York Times, March 16, 2019, p. A1. See also, Kevin Roose. "A Shooting Disturbingly Rooted in the Internet." *New York Times*, March 16, 2019, p. A-1, and Charlotte Graham-McLay, Damien Cave and Benjamin Mueller, "They Found a Haven From Strife, Only to Mourn." *New York Times*, March 16, 2019, p. A1.

[20] Jane Onyanga-Omara. U.S. Today, "New Zealand PM Vows Changes To Gun Laws." *New York Times*, March 18, 2019, p. 17A.

[21] John Bacon. "New Zealanders turn in guns in wake of attack." *Detroit Free Press*, March 19, 2019, p. 8A.

[22] Ian Austen, "After Mass Shooting, Canada Bans Assault Weapons," *New York Times*, May 2, 2020, p. A19.

[23] U.S. Const. Art. VI, cl. 3.

[24] Adel Hassan, "Parkland Survivors Unveil Plan on Guns," *New York Times*, August 22, 2019, p. A13.

[25] Alexander Burns, "Bloomberg, a Crusader Against Guns, Unveils a Detailed Action plan," *New York Times*, December 6, 2019, p. A21.

[26] *Heller*, 554 U.S. at 570 (citing 4 Blackstone 148–149 (1769)).

[27] 18 U.S.C. §§ 921-31 (Unlawful Acts); 26 U.S.C. § 5801-72 (Excise taxes on firearms and Registration of manufacturers and dealers).

[28] Michelle Singletary, "The enormous economic cost of gun violence." The *Washington Post*, Michelle Singletary on Twitter @ Singletary M and Facebook. Singletary writes the personal finance column, "The Color of Money" syndicated by The *Washington Post* Writers Group.

[29] Timothy Williams, Sabrina Tavernise, Zolan Kanno-Youngs and Sarah Mervosh, "Gun Rights Activists Amass in a Shifting State," *New York Times*, January 21, 2020, p. A1. Timothy Williams and Sabrina Tavernise, "Virginia Opposed Gun Limits, but a Population Shift Is Changing Minds," *New York Times*, January 31, 2020, p. A17.

[30] Paul Egan, (*Detroit Free Press* and USA Network), "Protestors crowd Capitol over state of emergency," *Detroit Free Press*, May 1, 2020, p. A4.

[31] Christine Hall, "Macomb gun rights sanctuary gains favor," *Detroit Free Press*, January 16, 2020, p. 1A.

ABOUT THE AUTHOR

DAVID L. NELSON was raised in Michigan's Upper Peninsula where hunting and target shooting are a way of life. He learned to shoot at an early age and listened to claims that the Second Amendment protected an individual's right to bear arms even before the Supreme Court declared that was the law.

After graduating from Northern Michigan University, he earned a juris doctor degree from the University of Michigan Law School in 1957. He is a member of the Michigan Bar Association and was accepted to the bar of the United States Supreme Court in 1973. He practiced law for more than forty years, specializing in commercial litigation before retiring in 2001. He is the author of two books: *Tool Marks Don't Lie* and *River of Iron*.

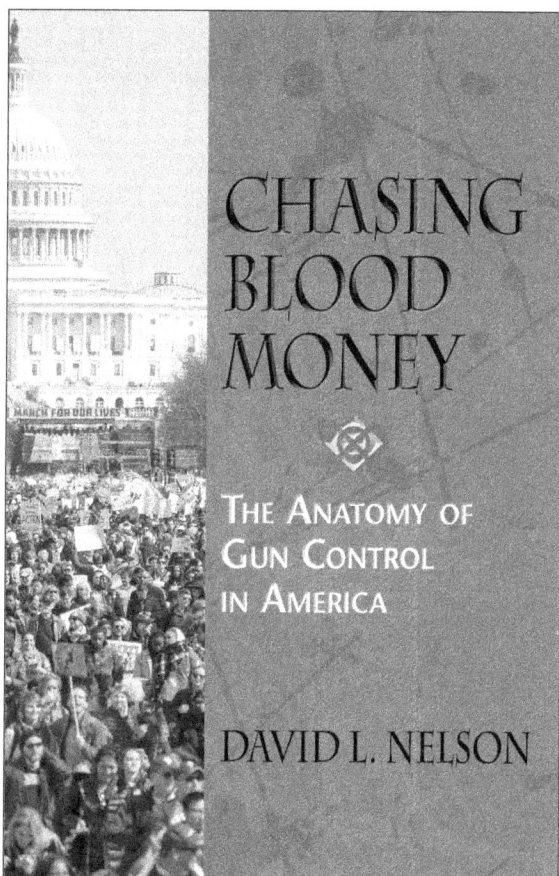

Chasing Blood Money

The Anatomy of Gun Control in America

David L. Nelson

Publisher: SDP Publishing

Also available in ebook format

 **SDP Publishing**

www.SDPPublishing.com

Contact us at: info@SDPPublishing.com

www.ingramcontent.com/pod-product-compliance
Lightning Source LLC
Chambersburg PA
CBHW060534210326
41519CB00014B/3217